JAPAN:
Why It Works,
Why It Doesn't

JAPAN:
Why It Works,
Why It Doesn't

Economics in
Everyday Life

EDITED BY
James Mak, Shyam Sunder,
Shigeyuki Abe, and Kazuhiro Igawa

A LATITUDE 20 BOOK
UNIVERSITY OF HAWAI'I PRESS
HONOLULU

03 02 01 00 99 98   5 4 3 2 1

Library of Congress Cataloging-in-Publication Data

Japan—why it works, why it doesn't :
  economics in everyday life / edited by
  James Mak . . . [et al.].
    p. cm.
  Includes bibliographical references and
  index.
ISBN 0–8248–1967–5 (alk. paper)
  1. Japan—Economic conditions—1945–
  2. Japan—Social life and customs—1945–
  3. National characteristics, Japanese.
  I. Mak, James.
  HC462.9.J327   1997
  330.952—dc21   97–21306
                                   CIP

University of Hawai'i Press books are printed
on acid-free paper and meet the guidelines
for permanence and durability of the Council
on Library Resources

Designed by David C. denBoer

CONTENTS

Preface   ix

Acknowledgments   xiii

Living

1. Do the Japanese Live Better Than Americans?   3
    Charles Yuji Horioka

2. Why Avoid the Altar?   11
    Andrew Mason and Naohiro Ogawa

3. Why Go to School after School?   21
    Shigeyuki Abe and Kazuhiro Igawa

4. Why So Many Gifts?   27
    Robert Parry

5. Why Is Pachinko So Popular?   33
    Shigeyuki Abe and James Mak

6. Why Are the Japanese Obsessed with
    Luxury Brand-Name Goods?   39
    Kazuo Nishiyama

7. Why Are There So Many Small Shops
    in Japan?   45
    James Mak and Shyam Sunder

8. How Do the Japanese and Americans
    Spend Their Money?   51
    James Mak

9.   How Can the Japanese Manage without
     Personal Checking Accounts?   59
     Toshiki Jinushi and James Mak

10. What Are Most Japanese Doing on Tax Day?   67
     Robert McCleery

Work

11. Why Do Students Take It Easy at the University?   73
     *Shigeyuki Abe, Shoji Nishijima, Shyam Sunder, and
     Karen Lupardus*

12. Why Do Japanese Companies Hire
     Only Spring Graduates?   83
     Teruyuki Higa

13. Why Don't Workers Claim All Their Overtime?   91
     Teruyuki Higa and Karen Lupardus

14. How Do Workers Get Paid?   99
     Naoki Mitani

15. Do the Japanese Work till They Drop?   107
     Yoshitaka Fukui

16. Why Do the Japanese Save So Much?   115
     Charles Yuji Horioka

System

17. Why Is Japan a Paradise of Vending Machines?   123
     Robert Parry

18. Why Do Doctors Prescribe So Many Pills?   131
     Akihiko Kawaura and Sumner LaCroix

19. Why Do Bank Automatic Teller Machines
     Shut Down at 7 P.M.?   137
     Shyam Sunder

Contents   vii

20. Why Is Rice So Expensive in Japan?   149
    Susumu Hondai

21. How Can the Japanese Spend So Little
    on Health Care?   157
    Matthew Loke and James Mak

22. How Does Japan's Largest Bank Work?   167
    Toshiki Jinushi

23. Why Do So Many Japanese Contribute
    to Public TV?   173
    Kazuhiro Igawa and James Mak

24. Why Are So Few People on Welfare in Japan?   179
    Yoko Kimura

25. What Are *Keiretsu* and Why Do Some
    U.S. Companies Dislike Them?   185
    Gary Kikuchi

26. Is Japan an Egalitarian Society?   195
    Harry Oshima

Glossary of Japanese Terms   205

Sources for Statistical Data on Japan   209

About the Contributors   211

Index   215

PREFACE

Japan has fascinated visitors for centuries. Historically, its ethnic homogeneity, isolation, and rugged terrain inspired a deep sense of community in its people. At the end of the twentieth century, Japan's thoroughly urbanized population lives in the coastal plains and travels to all corners of the globe, but the commitment to community persists. That, above all else, lies at the root of the continued fascination of foreigners with Japan, especially those who arrive with antipodean views where ruggedness is associated with individualism, not community.

Like most other visitors, two of us (Mak and Sunder), too, arrived in Japan with little understanding of this society. The cliché of "Western-style industrial democracy" framed what little we had learned and thought about Japan. You get off the plane in Narita thinking it's Heathrow, only with different faces and writing. But economists can hardly spend a day in Japan without their sense of order being assaulted from many directions. This is hardly unusual for foreign visitors to any land. An understanding of the local conditions helps render the strange and inexplicable phenomena understandable if not acceptable.

Our own visit to Japan was no exception. We started compiling a list of such phenomena and talked to just about anybody who would listen in our attempts to understand them in economic terms. What follows is the result of this expedition. Our teachers in this expedition were mostly our colleagues at Kobe University who sat through scores of lunch sessions, as we violated the Japanese etiquette of a quiet meal, badgering them with hundreds of questions about what we saw or thought we had seen.

Our hosts listened and answered our questions. They generously and frequently offered to gather more information and to introduce us to people who might know more. They politely corrected us when we failed to observe important parts of what was going on. Frequently we heard, "Oh, I have never thought about that question." It should not have surprised us, because visitors to the United States too have many questions its residents hardly ever think about.

For example, Japanese visitors to the United States are often bewildered by our practice of tipping waiters, bartenders, taxi drivers, barbers and hairdressers, hotel doormen, and so forth. Most Americans have never thought about why we tip in the United States, other than "It's expected." There is no tipping in Japan, yet service levels there are far higher than in the United States. However, our own surprise at our observations of Japan, inevitably involving comparisons with the United States, and the openness of our Japanese friends, encouraged us to write an account of what we learned. This book is the result of that joint endeavor of the visitors and their hosts (Abe and Igawa).

As we began to look into the issues, we soon discovered that each question was too deep and detailed for us to know enough to write about with authority and confidence. We solicited help from friends, in the United States and Japan, to do most of the writing. While the writing has been kept at an accessible level, the knowledge and expertise of those who wrote these pieces ensured that it has a firm base in fact and research.

The title of each essay takes the form of a simple question that encapsulates, as a starting point, the ignorance, prejudice, and overconfidence of visitors. Inevitably, visitors carry the baggage of their own norms and question the reasonableness of the differences they see. The stories start with some personal observations supplemented by hard data to establish the legitimacy of the question raised. A list of candidate explanations of the phenomenon is followed by discussion of their strengths, weaknesses, and credibility. Each essay strives for rational explanation, allowing for historical contingencies. We keep the discussion of irrational explanations to a minimum, largely because economists have little to contribute in that respect. At the end of the essay, the author frequently takes off the economist's hat, and joins the reader to offer his or her own personal opinion. This format affords the author the opportunity to take sides without his or her opinion being confused with the analysis.

We have kept the language simple and minimized the jargon of social sciences to keep the work accessible to general audiences. When technical terms cannot be avoided, we provide explanations immediately. We sacrifice rigor for readability.

The essays are organized into three loosely defined sections—Living, Work, and System. Most visitors are exposed to these aspects of Japanese society. We picked specific topics in these areas on the basis of our own curiosity. These topics can be considered a small, random sample at best. Any attempt at comprehensive coverage of Japanese economic institutions is well beyond the scope of this work. We deliberately excluded current economic issues such as U.S.-Japan trade disputes which have been widely reported and discussed in print and electronic media.

The bulk of the book's readers will consist of college and high-school students studying about Japan and a significant proportion of the educated public in the United States and elsewhere who have acquired more than a casual interest in Japan. Visitors to Japan may find a refreshing perspective in this book, both before as well as after their visit to this fascinating country. This perspective may help them organize their own visit and observations, and ultimately, understand Japan at a deeper level.

Stereotypes about Japan have proliferated with its economic power. Frederik L. Schodt eloquently describes four American views of Japan: friend, foe, model, and mirror. With its integration into the world economy, debunking false beliefs about Japan is not a mere luxury; it is a necessity. Americans have often talked about, and worked on, importing Japanese institutions. These essays by American and Japanese scholars, sometimes paired together, suggest that such borrowing would not necessarily be easy or effective.

The economic approach used here to address a small sample of questions is more important than the specific answers provided. In a fast-changing society, such specifics soon become obsolete or irrelevant. We have no illusions that these essays furnish the definitive answers to the questions raised. Our conversations with students, scholars, and other English-speaking visitors from Japan occasionally reveal their frustration with facile "cultural" explanations of Japan so popular in the press. In that mode of thinking, every difference in Japan becomes rooted in its special culture and tradition, and every attempt to understand the rational basis for the difference becomes an attack by outsiders who are insensitive to their own ethnocentrism.

Many special features of Japan do not survive the application of economic reasoning; the institutions examined in this book are also found elsewhere in Asia, Europe, or even in the United States, in similar or modified forms. Absence of personal checking accounts, large employee bonuses, large postal banks, and a special self-identity are examples of such phenomena. Economic institutions in Japan, like elsewhere, can be understood as rational responses to historical accidents. Perhaps these simple essays will trickle into Japan's rationalist current. Nothing will delight us more than to find a Japanese audience for this book.

ACKNOWLEDGMENTS

We have gathered many debts in this endeavor. Many friends and colleagues have contributed their precious time and expertise to write contributions to this volume, and persisted through several stages of editing and rewriting. Lucien Ellington, Christopher Grandy, David McClain, Allan Meltzer, Manjula Shyam, and Kozo Yamamura read through the entire manuscript and offered us detailed comments. In addition, Roger Blair, Byron Gangnes, Yuji Ijiri, Dai Kinoshita, Sumner LaCroix, Alice Mak, Frank Mak, Richa Shyam, Pat Steinhoff, and Hidetoshi Yamaji read some of the essays and shared their comments and reactions with us. Abe's fall 1996 class at the Stanford Japan Center in Kyoto used a preliminary version of this book, and Jason Eis sent us thoughtful comments at the end of the session. Charles Horioka was quick to supply us with information. Professor Akira Kajiwara and Takahiro Nakayama of Kobe University helped find and translate the original news sources for the essay on automatic teller machines. Without implicating them in errors that remain, we express our gratitude to all of them for helping us make this a better book.

James Mak's and Shyam Sunder's visits to Kobe University during the summer of 1995 that gave rise to this project were supported by the Ministry of Education (Monbusho), the Graduate School of International Co-operation Studies, and the Research Institute for Economics and Business Administration at Kobe University. On their return, their work on the book was financed by the Department of Economics, University of Hawaii at Manoa for Mak and Sunder, and by the Richard M. and Margaret Cyert Family Funds for Sunder.

We are delighted to have had the chance to work with William Hamilton, director of the University of Hawai'i Press, Cheri Dunn, managing editor, and other members of the Press staff to bring this project to a conclusion. Without Bill's strong encouragement, even before the idea for the work had fully taken shape, there would have been no book.

We owe a special debt to Karen Lupardus and Yoshitaka Fukui. Karen not only contributed two essays to this volume and prepared the glossary and index but her editorial skills also helped make this volume readable. Yoshi brought his tremendous knowledge of Japanese institutions and economic analysis to save us from sloppy reasoning and overgeneralization. He wrote one essay and provided us with numerous references and data to help sharpen many other essays. Frank Mak and James Mak supplied the cover photographs and Bryant Fukutomi and Matthew Loke provided the imaginative charts. Roger Dahl graciously permitted us to use his cartoons, which were first published in the *Japan Times*.

Professor Teruyuki Higa, who contributed two essays, passed away while this volume was being edited. A graduate of the University of Hawaii at Manoa, he received his Ph.D. in economics at the University of Illinois at Urbana-Champaign and then went on to become professor of economics at Okinawa International University. Dr. Higa always found great pleasure in eating, drinking, traveling, and sharing with others his unique personal observations about the places he visited. We hope the readers will find that same spirit of adventure in these pages. We lovingly dedicate this book to his memory.

JAPAN:
Why It Works,
Why It Doesn't

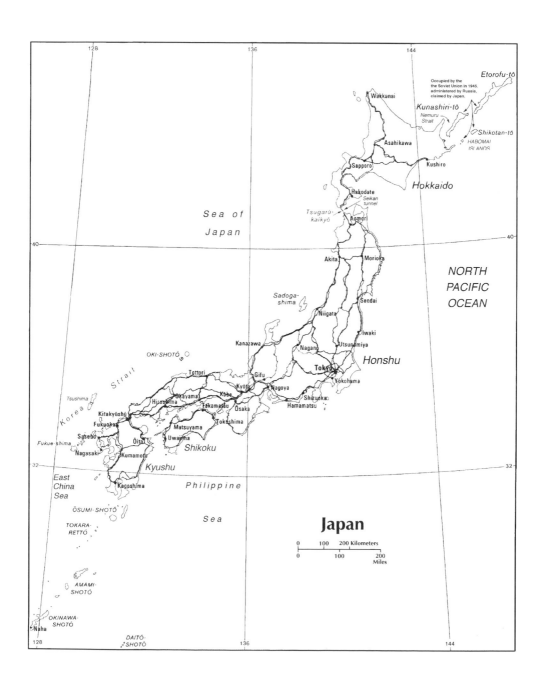

128   136   144

Occupied by the
the Soviet Union in 1945,
administered by Russia,
claimed by Japan.

Etorofu-tō

Kunashiri-tō

Nemuru
Strait

Shikotan-tō

HABOMAI
ISLANDS

Wakkanai

Asahikawa

Kushiro

Sapporo

Hokkaido

Hakodate

Seikan
tunnel

Tsugarū-
kaikyō

Aomori

Sea of

Japan

40 — — — — 40

Akita

Morioka

NORTH
PACIFIC
OCEAN

Sadoga-
shima

Sendai

Niigata

Iwaki

Kanazawa

Nagano

Utsunomiya

OKI-SHOTŌ

Tottori

Gifu

Tokyo

Honshu

Kyōto

Nagoya

Yokohama

Korea Strait

Tsushima

Okayama

Kōbe

Shizuoka

Hiroshima

Takamatsu

Ōsaka

Hamamatsu

Kitakyūshū

Fukuoka

Matsuyama

Tokushima

Fukue-shima

Sasebo

Ōita

Uwajima

Nagasaki

Kumamoto

Shikoku

East
China
Sea

Kyushu

Philippine

32 — 32

ŌSUMI-SHOTŌ

Kagoshima

TOKARA-
RETTŌ

Sea

Japan

0   100   200 Kilometers

0   100   200
Miles

AMAMI-
SHOTŌ

OKINAWA-
SHOTŌ

Naha

DAITŌ-
SHOTŌ

128   136   144

Living

1

Do the Japanese Live Better Than Americans?

Charles Yuji Horioka

Gross domestic product (GDP) per person is a common measure of a country's standard of living. It is simply the total value of all final goods and services produced in a certain economy within a given period of time (usually one year); per capita GDP is GDP divided by population.

Is Japan's per Capita GDP Higher Than That of the United States?

In 1995, the per capita GDP of Japan was 3,830,700 yen while the per capita GDP of the United States was 26,438 dollars.[1] The Japanese number is larger, but it is stated in Japanese currency. The two figures can be meaningfully compared only if they are both stated in the same monetary unit—either yen or dollars.

In 1995, a dollar could be exchanged for 94.06 yen on average. At this exchange rate, Japan's per capita GDP was 40,726 U.S. dollars. That was 54 percent higher than the per capita

---

[1] The yen–dollar exchange rate is continually changing. Unless indicated otherwise, throughout this book the yen–dollar exchange rate is arbitrarily set at 100 yen equal to one dollar.

GDP of the United States in the same year. Since 1995, the value of the Japanese yen has weakened considerably relative to the U.S. dollar (to about 115 yen to the dollar at this writing). If these more recent exchange rates were used to compare the per capita GDPs of the two countries, Japan's will be higher by about 25 percent. It would appear that the Japanese do in fact live better than Americans.

Are Market Exchange Rates Adequate for Comparing GDP Figures?

It would be appropriate to use market exchange rates to convert the Japanese per capita GDP figures to U.S. dollars if prices were about the same in the two countries or if the United States were right next to Japan so that Japanese consumers could do all of their shopping there. In reality, however, prices are much higher in Japan, and there is a wide ocean separating the two countries. As a result, it is not practical for Japanese consumers to go to the United States every time they need a loaf of bread or a carton of milk.

Japanese consumers sometimes do go abroad on shopping expeditions just to take advantage of the much lower prices and then return to Japan with suitcases full of designer-label clothes, accessories, cosmetics, and so on. These expeditions require a considerable amount of time, money, and effort. Customs duties must be paid on purchases in excess of the duty-free limit (currently at 2,000 U.S. dollars per person), and it is difficult if not impossible to bring back perishable, heavy, or bulky goods. Under the circumstances, using market exchange rates to convert Japanese GDP figures to U.S. dollars is not adequate for a fair comparison of the GDP figures for the two countries. The appropriate exchange rate to use is one that takes account of price differences between the two countries.

Careful calculations by the Paris-based Organization for Economic Co-operation and Development (OECD) show that on average prices in Japan were 1.8686 times those in the United States in 1995. This number is only an average. Price differences were even greater in the case of certain goods and services. For example, furniture, floor coverings, and repairs were 3.5 times more expensive in Japan; meat, 3.3 times more expensive; bread/cereals, footwear (including repairs), and recreational and cultural services, 3.1 times more expensive; and the operation of transport equipment, 3.0 times more expensive. Only communication, medical and health care, individual government services, and tobacco were cheaper in Japan.

Converted at the market rate of exchange, the per capita GDP of Japan in 1995 was equivalent to 40,726 U.S. dollars. This dollar figure must be divided by the factor of 1.8686 in order to take into account the higher prices in Japan. Dividing $40,726 by 1.8686 yields $21,795, meaning that the per capita GDP of Japan in 1995 was, with this adjustment, actually *lower* than that of the United States—in fact, 17.6 percent lower.

Looked at another way, in 1995, it took 175.76 Japanese yen to buy in Japan what one U.S. dollar could buy in the United States. Thus, the yen-denominated per capita GDP of Japan in 1995 must be divided by 175.76 in order to determine how many U.S. dollars would be needed to buy goods and services in the United States compared to what the per capita GDP of Japan could buy in Japan in 1995. The answer again is 21,795 U.S. dollars. Japan's per capita GDP is considerably lower than that of the United States if price differences between the two countries are taken into account. The comparison of per capita GDP in the two countries, after accounting for price differences, suggests that Americans have a higher standard of living.

How Does Japan Compare with the United States in Other Aspects of the Standard of Living?

Per capita GDP alone is a very incomplete measure of the standard of living. A proper measure must include many factors other than the goods and services produced and consumed. For example, comparing figures for GDP tells us nothing about such factors as leisure time, social infrastructure, housing conditions, and social conditions, all of which contribute to a country's standard of living. What other aspects must we consider in our comparison of standards of living?

Leisure Time

Japanese workers spend more hours at work, and in traveling to work, than American workers. Consequently, they have less time for leisure. In 1993–1994, average annual working hours of Japanese workers fell for the first time slightly below the U.S. average (1,966 versus 1,976), but that was only because the United States had a relatively strong economy and Japan had a poor economy that year. Besides, those figures are not a true comparison because the Japanese figures do not include "service overtime" or unpaid overtime (see chapter 13). In addition to spending more time at work, the Japanese workers also spend more time getting to and from their jobs. The average commuting times in Japan are far longer than in the United States, not uncommonly one-and-a-half to two hours each way for workers in the major metropolitan areas.

Social Infrastructure

Japan also lags behind the United States in per capita amounts of social infrastructure such as roads, ports, airports, sewage and water systems, parks, and the like. For example, in comparison with U.S. cities, Japan's cities have only about one-tenth the amount of park acreage per person. Only 51 percent of Japanese homes are connected to sewage systems and 76 percent have flush toilets compared to 73 and 98 percent respectively in the United States. In terms of social infrastructure, Japan leaps ahead of the United States only in the availability of good public transportation. Although often overcrowded, Japanese trains, subways, and buses generally offer clean, frequent, convenient, and incredibly punctual service.

Housing Conditions

Housing conditions in Japan are generally far below those in the United States despite the fact that housing prices and rents are much higher in Japan (see chapter 8). For example, floor space per person in Japan is comparable to Western Europe but less than half that in the United States (31 versus 63 square meters), and central heating is virtually unheard of in Japan.

Social Conditions

Japanese also fare worse than Americans with respect to consumer protection, employment discrimination against women and the elderly, welfare programs for the poor, suicide rates, and earthquakes and other natural disasters (e.g., typhoons).

The amount by which the Japanese standard of living falls short of that in the United States would be even greater than their per capita GDP figures suggest if the amounts and quality of leisure time, social infrastructure, housing conditions, and social conditions were taken into account. The few favorable aspects for Japan, such as public transportation, can hardly outweigh the country's deficiencies in these areas.

However, there are other aspects of the standard of living in which Japan does far better than the United States. Most important, perhaps, is the fact that Japan has relatively less crime and lower unemployment. Japan also can boast of lower infant mortality rates, less family income inequality, fewer personal bankruptcies, a lower divorce rate, fewer teenage pregnancies, longer life expectancy, and better health insurance. Taking account of these factors would certainly narrow the gap between Japan and the United States, but this would not, in my opinion, change the verdict: the Japanese do *not* live better than Americans; in fact, they are considerably worse off.

Of course, I do not mean to belittle the phenomenal performance of the Japanese economy during the postwar period. Japan's per capita GDP was only 30.9 percent of U.S. per capita GDP in 1960 (after adjusting for price differences). From the mid-1950s to the early 1970s, the Japanese economy grew at double-digit rates to narrow the per capita GDP gap to a mere 82.4 percent of the United States by 1995. Although Japan has not caught up with the United States, most of the gap was closed in a mere thirty-five years. That's pretty impressive given how far behind Japan was to begin with.

What Can Be Done to Improve Japan's Standard of Living?

What can Japan do to further decrease the gap in living standards in comparison with the United States? The most effective way would be to further close the gap in their per capita GDP. This could be done in one of two ways. One way is for Japan to achieve faster economic growth than the United States. The other way is for Japan to lower its domestic prices. The second way is probably a better and more feasible choice.

In my opinion, Japanese prices are higher primarily because of import restrictions and government regulations. Opening up the Japanese market to imports and abolishing or relaxing government regulations would be an effective way to lower prices. This could not be done in the past because the interest groups that benefited the most from import restrictions and government regulations were politically the most powerful (producers, especially farmers; see chapter 20) while those who were hurt the most were the least powerful (consumers).

In recent years, however, the United States and many of Japan's other trading partners have become increasingly antagonistic and critical about Japan's persistent trade surpluses and

The good life

Most Japanese adults are satisfied with their standard of living. Here is the breakdown.

Satisfied/more or less satisfied
72.7%

Dissatisfied/some-what dissatisfied
24.6%

Source: Ministry of Foreign Affairs, Bulletin No. 39, September 14, 1995

have therefore been putting pressure on Japan to lower these surpluses by reducing or eliminating import restrictions and government regulations (see chapter 7). This pressure from abroad *(gaiatsu)* has finally enabled the Japanese government to overcome domestic opposition to the reduction, or elimination, of import restrictions and government regulations. As a result of these governmental reforms, Japanese consumers will surely be better off.

In addition, Japan's standard of living can be brought closer to that of the United States by shortening work hours, improving social infrastructure and housing conditions, strengthening consumer protection and employment discrimination laws, expanding services and facilities for the handicapped, and providing more generous welfare programs for the poor (see chapter 24). To their credit, the Japanese have been making improvements in most of these areas and, as a result, can expect to live much better in the future.

2

Why Avoid the Altar?

Andrew Mason and Naohiro Ogawa

The decline in marriage and the disintegration of the traditional family are some of the most widely discussed changes affecting U.S. society. By comparison, Japan seems to be a country of remarkable social stability. But surprisingly, the status of marriage is changing even more rapidly in Japan than in the United States and men and women are marrying even later. In 1995, 66 percent of men and 49 percent of women in their late twenties were single. In the United States, the corresponding figures (in 1990) were 46 percent for men and 32 percent for women. Singaporeans and Japanese now marry at a later age than anyone else in the world. (In several Northern European countries, marriage occurs at a later age, but only if consensual unions, which are widespread, are not counted as marriages.)

This is a radical change for a society in which marriage has been the norm. Among older generations, 99 percent of men and 98 percent of women have been married at some time during their lives. As younger generations increasingly choose to postpone tying the knot, the question becomes: "Will many Japanese forego marriage altogether?"

The Meaning of Marriage

Understanding the decline of marriage in Japan requires some understanding about what it means to be married and how

11

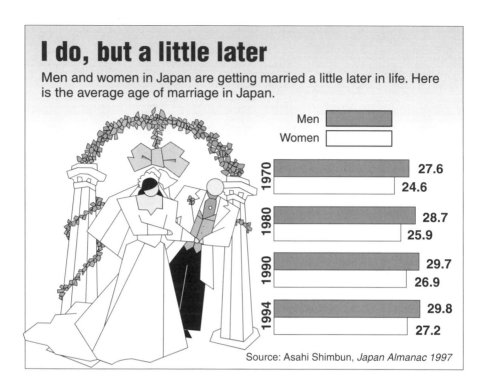

I do, but a little later

Men and women in Japan are getting married a little later in life. Here is the average age of marriage in Japan.

Men
Women

	Men	Women
1970	27.6	24.6
1980	28.7	25.9
1990	29.7	26.9
1994	29.8	27.2

Source: Asahi Shimbun, *Japan Almanac 1997*

married life in Japan differs from married life in the West. There are, of course, commonalities between the two societies. However, when a young Japanese woman decides to marry she is undertaking commitments and obligations that are very different from those a young American woman might expect. These differences fall into three roles: wife, mother, and daughter-in-law.

First, her role as wife to her future husband is likely to reflect a different kind of relationship from that found in American marriages. In Japan, there is less emphasis on marital companionship and sharing, and Japanese women depend less on their relationship with their husbands for emotional satisfaction. Arranged marriages are no longer common in Japan, but romantic love plays a less important role in courtship and marriage.

In part, the relationship between husbands and wives is a product of specialization. The typical Japanese husband is the quintessential breadwinner. He works long hours, stays out late, and is rarely involved in child rearing and housekeeping activities. According to the most recent international time budget study, Japanese men aged twenty to fifty-nine devoted only twenty minutes a day to household activities such as cooking, cleaning, shopping, or child care. By contrast, American men spent more than two hours a day helping around the house.

Second, a Japanese woman's role as mother is different from an American woman's in important respects. For most Japanese women, the most essential relationship is between herself and her children. Childless marriages are less common in Japan than in the United States. A high percentage of Japanese women begin childbearing shortly after marriage, have two children, and then stop. Unlike in the United States, births outside marriage are rare. For Japanese women, being married and rearing children are more synonymous than for American women.

Third, when a Japanese woman marries, she takes on important responsibilities as a daughter-in-law. Japan is a patrilineal society. When a woman marries, she becomes part of her husband's family. If she marries an eldest son, she and her husband, by tradition, live with his parents and she assists her mother-in-law in running the household. She also becomes the primary caregiver if and when her husband's parents reach old age. These traditions have weakened over time and more elderly Japanese are now living independently from their children. Still, when a Japanese woman marries, she is more likely than her American counterpart to live with her husband's parents, and she can expect to devote much more time and effort providing care to her husband's parents than most American women would ever dream of.

One other important aspect of marriage in Japan is its enduring nature. Divorce rates are much lower than in America.

"Till death do us part" may not be part of the marriage ceremony in Japan, but it is part of marriage.

Reasons for the Delay

A number of fundamental changes are affecting women's attitudes toward marriage. First, rapid economic and social change in Japan has had a profound impact on the opportunities for women outside marriage. As the Japanese economy has grown, job opportunities for women have multiplied. As employment in light industry and service sectors has increased, the economic returns to physical strength have declined relative to the returns to intelligence, dexterity, and other human characteristics that women possess in abundance. Women have benefited from increased opportunities for schooling and so the difference in educational attainment between men and women has steadily declined. As a consequence of these changes, the jobs available to women and the wages they are paid have steadily improved. Women can afford to forego marriage, and, to the extent that marriage and work are incompatible, the costs of marrying have substantially increased.

Why don't women choose to have their cake and eat it, too, by marrying and continuing to work? To some extent they do just that. In 1966, nearly 80 percent of single working women quit their jobs at the time of their marriage. Currently, about half the single working women continue to work, but the other half immediately withdraw from the labor force at the time of their marriage. There are a number of hard realities that reinforce traditional expectations about married women in Japan.

The first is the burden of child rearing, especially helping their children deal successfully with an extraordinarily competitive educational system. The Japanese accord a high priority to education, which is compulsory through junior high school. Ninety-six percent continue on to senior high school, and, of high school graduates, about 40 percent attend junior colleges or universities. Admission to the best schools, seen by parents as the key to success for their children, is determined by examination. To prepare for the do-or-die entrance examinations, a large proportion of Japanese children attend after-class private cram schools called *juku* (see chapter 3). In 1993, about 24 percent of elementary school students and 60 percent of junior high students studied at *juku*, and the percentages have been rising in recent years.

Japanese mothers are responsible for closely supervising homework assigned by both their children's *juku* and their regular school. If the children don't do well in school, the blame falls first on the mother. Of course, when the children do well, the mother also gets most of the credit. Being an "education mother" *(kyōiku-mama)* carries social prestige for many married women, but in a recent survey, approximately 55 percent of married women agreed that child rearing involves a great deal of anxiety over the education of their children. The additional schooling also imposes a financial burden—a quarter of working women report that their main reason for working was to earn money for their children's educational expenses.

Second, the Japanese tax code, social security system, and the policies of private companies also reinforce the incompatibility of marriage and work for women. A wife who earns in excess of 1.03 million yen (about 10,300 U.S. dollars) loses her dependent status and has to pay her own social security taxes and health insurance costs. Her husband faces the loss of company-provided spousal benefits. Because of such financial disincentives, many married women who do work opt for part-time employment. Of course, in this regard, two-income couples in the United States may feel similarly penalized by both the tax code (i.e., the "marriage penalty") and the policies of some employers.

However, the choice women face is more clear-cut in Japan than in the United States. They can marry, have children, and maybe work part-time; or they can postpone marriage, live with their parents, keep their jobs, and enjoy a considerable degree of economic and personal freedom. Many are choosing the latter option. It is increasingly common to see young single Japanese women vacationing in Hawaii, Australia, and Europe—a sight that would have been rare indeed twenty years ago.

The rise in educational attainment of women also may be having a more direct impact on marriage. In the United States, husbands and wives typically have similar levels of educational attainment. In Japan, husbands are traditionally more educated than their wives. This presented no problem when educational achievement among men was generally much higher than among women. But as the educational gap between men and women has narrowed, poorly educated men and highly educated women have found it increasingly difficult to find marriage partners who fit the traditional education pattern. Although men and women could adjust and marry partners more nearly their equal, this change has yet to occur.

The Burden of Caring for the Elderly

A second fundamental change that may be undermining the attractiveness of marriage is demographic in origin. Japan is the most rapidly aging society in the world. Its life expectancy exceeds that of any other country. But the declining percentage of young people and the increasing percentage of old people also reflect the decline in childbearing (and the decline in marriage). Providing care for the elderly may be particularly acute because the numbers of the very old are growing so rapidly. The nature and severity of many problems, such as senile dementia, increase very rapidly after age eighty. Thus, the demands placed on the primary caregiver can be substantial.

Institutionalization of the elderly is less accepted in Japan than in the United States (see chapter 21). There are fewer nursing homes and fewer retirement communities designed to meet the special needs of the elderly. Consequently, the responsibility for providing care falls more directly on the shoulders of children, even if parents and their children are living separately.

Because the birthrate has declined substantially in Japan, caring for elderly parents is shared among fewer siblings. If the responsibility falls exclusively on daughters-in-law, about half of those with an elderly parent-in-law will bear sole responsibility. Is the prospect of spending years caring for a husband's aging parents discouraging women from marrying? Perhaps not. But in the absence of the development of new institutional arrangements, providing such care will increasingly dominate the lives of women in their fifties and sixties. That such caregiving would affect attitudes toward marriage seems likely.

The High Monetary Cost of Marriage

A third factor that may be affecting marriage is to be found in the direct financial costs of the wedding, and the logistics and expenses involved in acquiring a place to live and setting up a household. In the United States, one of the first issues any young couple faces is housing. Most young couples initially rent an apartment. A few who are well off buy a condominium or a house, often with the help of their parents. Thus, the affordability of housing is a major issue in the marriage decision, particularly in high-cost urban areas.

The picture is a little more complicated in Japan. Housing is far more expensive (see chapter 8). Compared to Americans, the average Japanese household spends about 50 percent more of its household budget on housing, even though the typical Japanese housing unit is much smaller and the typical commute is much longer.

A mitigating factor is that young Japanese couples have an alternative to renting an exorbitantly high-priced apartment— they can remain at home. In 1990, the last year for which data are available, about 25 percent of married couples in their late twenties and 30 percent of couples in their thirties lived with relatives.

Although living with one's parents is an option for many more Japanese than American couples, behavior is changing rapidly in Japan. Young adults are much more likely to live apart from their parents, and, as attitudes change, the cost of housing no doubt looms larger in the marriage decision than it once did.

Before paying for an apartment, the couple must pay for the cost of a wedding, which can be a major financial undertaking in Japan. Weddings, especially the elaborate dinner-party receptions, are extraordinarily expensive. The average cost of a wedding was 3.3 million yen (about 33,000 U.S. dollars) in 1995, and the honeymoon averaged another 900,000 yen (9,000 U.S. dollars). The cost of an American wedding pales by comparison. Not surprisingly, each year thousands of Japanese couples travel to Hawaii to get married. The total cost of the trip, including expenses for seven guests, is less than 2 million yen, still a substantial sum.

The decision to defer marriage in Japan is part of a broader change in the fundamental role of the family. More and more young Japanese men and women are living alone prior to marriage. Those who have married are spending a far shorter portion of their adult lives rearing children than was true of their parents. And those who are reaching old age are much less likely to live with and depend on their children for old age support than was true a generation ago. Under these rapidly changing circumstances, it is no wonder that young Japanese women and men are reassessing the role that marriage should play in their lives.

3

Why Go to School after School?

Shigeyuki Abe and Kazuhiro Igawa

In Japan, it is not unusual to see groups of young schoolchildren riding trains or walking along city streets as late as 10 P.M. on school days. What are these young people doing out so late? They are going home, tired after spending long evening hours at their after-school private cram schools known as *juku*. They can often be seen buying vitamin-enriched stamina drinks, a product initially targeted at exhausted "salarymen" (the Japanese term for male office workers) seeking a quick energy recharge.

The Ministry of Education (Monbusho) reported that in fiscal year 1993, 36.4 percent of elementary and junior high school students attended *juku* after their regular school hours. Among third-year junior high school students (i.e., ninth-graders), 70 percent attended *juku*. Even among first-graders, the percentage of students attending *juku* had risen to 12 percent. Today in Tokyo, there are about 150 cram schools catering to preschool children whose parents hope to enroll the youngsters in elite private kindergartens and elementary schools. Why do so many Japanese children go to *juku* after their regular school?

The Japanese Education System

Japan has maintained a high regard for education throughout its history. Hierarchy and educational credentialism (the importance of "prestige") have long been common themes in Japanese education.

For generations, Japan has recognized that money spent on education provides both a "social" and a "private" return. The social return derives from the fact that a more educated citizenry leads to a better society. The private return derives from the higher income and other personal benefits that an individual receives from more schooling. In Japan, universal primary education is believed to yield high social benefits, which decline at higher levels of education. On the other hand, the private benefits continue to rise with more schooling. These principles are behind the design of Japan's modern education system.

In 1900, free public education was introduced. In 1947, the Fundamental Law of Education mandated nine years of universal public schooling for both boys and girls. Beyond the ninth grade, the government subsidizes a declining percentage of additional education. Public high school enrollment is restricted in Japan so that, today, only 40 percent of all high school students attend public school. To make up for the shortage of public high school openings, a large private school system has evolved. As a result, 95 percent of junior high school graduates go on to high school. Some private schools today have more prestige than their public competitors, which used to be thought most prestigious. In higher education, public universities only accommodate 28 percent of college students. The decline of subsidies to education beyond the ninth grade is a deliberate policy that recognizes that benefits of education shift from the community level to private individuals at higher levels of education.

Why Attend *Juku?*

Given these educational spending priorities, it is not surprising that at the end of ninth grade, Japanese children compete hard to capture one of the limited number of spaces at the public high schools. Entry is determined strictly by merit on the basis of performance on standardized entrance examinations.

Japanese schools are remarkably similar in their curriculum and status until the high school level, when the status and prestige of the school become important in determining a student's future opportunities. Attendance at a respected high school improves a student's chances for entry into a prestigious university, which in turn, enhances the student's career opportunities and marriage prospects. Moreover, the school uniform that the student wears, particularly in the case of girls, announces to the public that the parents have succeeded, or failed, to get their youngster into a good school. Not surprisingly, students are pressured to perform well on the competitive entrance examinations. The same pressures are repeated, of course, when the time comes to apply for university admission. In this hierarchical educational system, it is easy to understand why parents send their children to *juku*. This has become particularly true as the *juku* have increasingly shifted their focus away from complementing regular school lessons to the sole task of preparing students for entrance examinations.

Parents have other reasons to send their children to *juku*. The extra schooling instills a disciplined work ethic in children beginning at an early age. Many parents feel that the whole examination process, while stressful for their children, is good preparation for life. Also, most *juku* tend to have smaller classes, allowing greater flexibility in teaching methods. This is important because class size in public schools is large, typically forty pupils in the secondary schools, and also Japanese schools generally have no "accelerated" (or "decelerated") classes. Until recently, Japanese schools held classes for half a day on Saturdays, but now classes meet only two Saturdays each month, and some parents choose to send their children to *juku* to keep them occupied and out of trouble on the other Saturdays. The percentage of students attending *juku* has increased over the years.

Juku is not cheap. The average annual tuition for a sixth-grader is 2,000 U.S. dollars, and rising rapidly. A quarter of the working women in Japan report that their main reason for working is to help pay the educational expenses for their children. The *juku* industry has grown to become a trillion-yen (10-billion U.S. dollar) industry in Japan, about twice what it was ten years ago. Increasingly, children from lower-income families are being priced out of attending *juku* by the rising tuition. This could become an important factor in decreasing social mobility in Japan.

Interestingly, Japanese children generally support their parents' decision to send them to *juku*. A recent census survey finds that 70 percent of sixth- and ninth-graders believe that they must attend *juku*. They believe that it helps them in their regular schoolwork by giving them a chance to repeat some of the same material. *Juku* may also offer material before it is presented in school so that students can understand it more easily when they encounter it in class where, of course, they are given grades. And for many children whose friends attend *juku*, the cram school is also a place to socialize with classmates after school.

Does attending *juku* increase a student's chances of gaining admission to a desired school? It's hard to tell. Parents who have money and motivation tend to send their children to *juku*. Because so many students attend *juku*, it is difficult to assess the cost-effectiveness when you can't compare the achievement of the students who attend *juku* against a comparable cohort of students of equal abilities who don't attend *juku*. Moreover, as the percentage of students attending *juku* rises, the better schools are simply forced to raise their admission standards to ration the limited number of vacancies among the applicants. Most researchers believe that attending *juku* helps some students gain admission to better schools, if not the best schools.

If attending *juku* might not increase a student's chances of gaining admission to a prestigious school, does it add to the student's knowledge? Some people believe that *juku* students take their regular schoolwork less seriously, knowing that they will have a second chance to learn the material at *juku*. Some

people are concerned that by placing excessive emphasis on preparing students to take entrance examinations, *juku* may encourage rote memorization rather than creative and independent thinking.

Negative Effects

The negative consequences of sending children to long hours of after-school cram schools are increasingly visible. *Juku* is the symbol of the pressures students experience in taking entrance examinations. The recent rise in psychological problems among Japanese students has been attributed to these pressures. Junior high school absenteeism (of over fifty days per year) for reasons other than sickness or finances, has shown a steady rise over the past twenty years. School violence, often in the form of hazing known as *ijime,* has become common in Japanese schools. "School refusal syndrome" (students simply do not show up at school) has also become common. Others feel that *juku* destroys the students' curiosity and interest in learning and produces robot-like children who will study only when they are forced to.

These negative consequences can be ameliorated by deemphasizing the current entrance examinations as the sole criterion in the school admission process in favor of a broader set of criteria that includes individual creativity, interest, leadership, and other personal traits. This action has been recommended by the Ministry of Education and is currently being implemented. It is hoped that this will give back to the young their childhood, allow them to pursue a broader range of interests, and encourage the development of individual diversity. If the pressures of educational advancement could be reduced or delayed, Japan would be able to raise happy, not tired and stressed-out, children.

4

Why So Many Gifts?

Robert Parry

The doorbell rings; you open the door to receive a beautifully wrapped parcel from one of Japan's prestigious department stores. What is it? Excitement fills the air as you carefully remove the wrapping paper—nobody tears open parcels in Japan—to reveal . . . several months' supply of laundry detergent. Congratulations! You are at the receiving end of the Japanese custom of giving seasonal gifts.

The Japanese also give presents when they travel, and on other special occasions. Larger stores in Japan have sections devoted solely to gifts. At tourist destinations around the globe, you also see many Japanese buying presents. It is not unusual for a Japanese family to spend over 100,000 yen (1,000 U.S. dollars) a year on presents.

Seasonal Gifts

Midsummer and the end of the year are the two major seasons for giving gifts. The practice has survived although its religious origins have faded. The midsummer gift, *ochūgen* (less formally, *chūgen*), originated from a combination of a Chinese Taoist ceremony and Japan's Buddhist bon festival. During this mid-August festival, the Japanese offer special dishes at small altars in their homes for the returning spirits of their ancestors. Today,

27

the largely urban population braves colossal traffic jams to return to its rural roots to enjoy local village festivities. The custom of making offerings to ancestors during the bon festival has been extended to giving presents to customers, supervisors, and others of higher rank, or to persons who have provided special favors in the past.

Similarly, December's year-end gifts, known as *oseibo* (also less formally called *seibo*), originated in offerings to the returning spirits of ancestors and gods at the New Year. Japanese companies do their part by paying summer and winter bonuses to their employees during these gift-giving seasons (see chapter 14). An average household sends about eight *chūgen* and eight *seibo* presents of about 4,000 yen (40 U.S. dollars) each. Consumables such as beer, instant coffee, soap, and laundry detergent are among the most popular gifts.

Travel-related Gifts

Souvenir gifts, or *omiyage*, are expected to be brought back from a trip and given to family, friends, and colleagues. The practice originated from pilgrimages to the main Japanese Shinto shrine, located at Ise in central Japan. In the past, few could afford the slow, treacherous, and costly trip. An entire community or village would contribute a send-off gift of money, called *senbetsu*, to help pay for one person to visit the shrine on behalf of all. The pilgrims would later return with good-luck charms known as *omamori* and other souvenirs as presents from the shrine for the contributors.

Today, travel destinations are more diverse, and the souvenir presents, known as *omiyage*, typically include purchases from luxury and duty-free shops abroad. The most popular gifts from domestic destinations are foodstuffs, usually cakes or sweets, that are famous products of the places visited. Buying these presents at shops in railway stations and airports before returning home minimizes the inconvenience of carrying the *omiyage* around

during the trip itself. Gift shops are stocked with prewrapped packages in various sizes to suit the purchaser, who might, for example, be looking for just the right number of tidbits for a specific number of co-workers. On average, a Japanese takes 1.5 domestic trips per year and spends over 6,500 yen (65 U.S. dollars) on *omiyage* per trip. The practice of giving *omiyage* has been extended to overseas trips, as anyone who has seen Japanese tourists in Honolulu's Ala Moana Shopping Center or in brand-name stores elsewhere, such as London's Fortnum and Mason, can testify (see chapter 6).

Rites of Passage

In Japan, as elsewhere, giving gifts is an important part of various rites of passage. There are manuals, some four hundred pages long, which describe the proper etiquette and procedures for various ceremonies and gifts. Weddings and funerals are occasions for the most elaborate forms of gift-giving.

Japanese weddings are lavish and expensive, usually costing several million yen (tens of thousands of U.S. dollars; see chapter 2). Seeing how these extravaganzas are financed reveals their ritual as well as practical sides. On being invited to a wedding, guests consult a manual to learn where to sit during the ceremony and subsequent dinner, and what gift would be appropriate. Only cash is given, discreetly enclosed in a specially decorated, elaborate envelope. The amount given depends on the wealth and status of the giver and where the wedding and reception take place. For many people, number "3," being odd and indivisible, symbolizes the bond of the couple, and so three 10,000 yen bills (300 U.S. dollars) might be given in the envelope. On the practical side, the cash gift helps pay for the food and other expenses of the wedding reception, including the standardized gift (often a plate) given to guests as they leave. This custom, whereby guests help cover the cost of the wedding reception, has led to more and more extravagant receptions, all to the delight of the companies that sell wedding packages and the luxury hotels where such receptions are often held.

At funerals, condolences are expressed by depositing about 3,000 yen (30 U.S. dollars) in a specially decorated envelope, which is received when guests arrive at the funeral. Upon departure, each person is presented with a gift, usually a handkerchief or small towel, and recently something additional such as a pen set, a packet of green tea, or even a prepaid telephone card, all properly wrapped for the occasion and worth approximately a thousand yen.

Status Value

The majority (90 percent) of Japanese consider themselves to be middle-class. The middle-class ethic manifests itself in concern with status, ranking of schools and companies, and attraction to brand names (see chapter 6). Gift-giving is linked to status and form in social relationships. It strengthens mutual ties and obligations between givers and recipients. The giving of presents indicates status. Giving *omiyage* indicates that you have enough money and knowledge to travel; your seasonal gifts of beer and soap wrapped in expensive gift-wrap marked with the logo of a famous department store demonstrate that you can afford to shop there and that you know the rules of the game. These features of middle-class behavior are hardly unique to Japan.

Consumable Goods

Gifts of cash and consumables (e.g., beer and soap) minimize waste. Consumables are used up quickly so they don't clutter the house. On the other hand, if you receive a clock that you don't care for from an aunt, you have to keep it and put it on display when she visits some months later. Not so with consumables. If you receive more soap than you want to keep, you can simply give it to someone else. This practice is known as *taraimawashi*. Or, you can sell the unwanted presents to businesses that specialize in the resale of gifts.

Mutual Ties

Giving presents reinforces mutual ties between companies (*keiretsu* or affiliated company groups), between employers and employees, businesses and customers, and among colleagues. The Japanese concept of *giri*—a moral imperative to carry out one's duty to the other members of one's groups—includes both reciprocity and indebtedness. As the recipient of a gift, a person is informed of being included in the sender's group as well as the mutual obligation to return the favor. Recipients of cash at weddings and funerals are expected to give small gifts in return; *chūgen* and *seibo* presents are exchanged between members of the same group; and *omiyage* are given in return for *senbetsu*. On Valentine's Day, women give *giri choco* (duty chocolate) to their male colleagues, who reciprocate by sending confectionery to their female colleagues on March 14, "White

Day." Such individually oriented gift-giving, popular among the younger generation, follows practices imported from the West.

The payback, however, need not be in the form of a tangible gift. Small business owners send presents to their clients with the expectation of assuring continued business. Office workers give gifts to their bosses and colleagues as an expression of their regard for them. Supervisors give gifts to their subordinates for the sake of harmony *(chōwa)*. In team-oriented Japanese organizations, harmony of the group is essential to its effectiveness. Patients give hefty monetary gifts—as much as 500,000 yen (5,000 U.S. dollars)—to their surgeons before operations to show appreciation for (hopefully) successful operations (see chapter 21).

The More Things Change . . .

Postwar urbanization and increasing mobility of employees across companies and of customers across suppliers are beginning to erode Japan's tightly knit system of mutual obligations. Nonetheless, gift-giving is but one manifestation of Japanese social fabric that remains strong. As in the West, Japanese retailers are only too happy to promote and reinforce the gift-giving culture on all possible occasions.

5

Why Is Pachinko
So Popular?

Shigeyuki Abe and James Mak

Pachinko, the Japanese version of the pinball machine, is one of the most popular leisure activities in Japan. Fifty percent of the Japanese have played it. In 1995, over 28 million Japanese played pachinko, an average of nearly twenty-five times during the year. Foreigners, seeing the Japanese sitting for hours in front of pachinko machines, often wonder what is so fascinating about this seemingly repetitive and monotonous game, and many Japanese would agree with that sentiment. Nonetheless, pachinko is big business in Japan.

There are over 18,000 pachinko parlors across the country, with 4.6 million pachinko machines. Pachinko parlors are concentrated in high-pedestrian-traffic areas near train and subway stations, shopping arcades, and malls, often right next to each other. Many are owned by Korean nationals living in Japan. In 1995, the Japanese spent an estimated 300 billion U.S. dollars playing pachinko—about 6 times the amount the country spent on national defense.

What Is Pachinko?

Pachinko is the Japanese adaptation of an American children's toy called the Corinthian Game, a flat board dotted with pins and holes. A ball is launched upward through a slot on the right side and allowed to roll back down, hitting the nails and possibly falling into a hole. Soon after the game was imported into Japan in 1924, local entrepreneurs quickly adapted it to stand vertically to save space, covered it with glass, and began to offer prizes to winners. Shortly thereafter the game became very popular among adults. The game was named "pachinko" after the "*pachi- pachi-*" sound of the metal balls hitting against the glass cover.

The first licensed pachinko parlor was opened in Nagoya City in 1930. During World War II, pachinko parlors were shut down, but they quickly reopened after the war. During those difficult years, players could even win rationed or luxury goods. The parlors probably procured these goods from the black market through organized crime connections, a relationship that is still believed to exist.

To play pachinko, you sit on a stool in front of the machine and launch a small 11 millimeter steel ball (about the size of the tip of your little finger) up the slot into the playing field using a mechanical spring-loaded driver. On its way down, the metal ball bounces among the pins and hits various targets. If it falls into a hole, you win—more shining balls cascade noisily out of the machine, just like a payoff at a Las Vegas slot machine. If you win large numbers of pachinko balls, you can exchange them for popular prizes such as cigarettes.

Like the old pinball machines, pachinko machines are eye-catching, with names like Airplane Pachinko, Fever Pachinko, Video Fever Pachinko, and Pachi-slo, which is a replica of the slot machine. The industry sustains customer interest by frequently introducing new games, and the machines themselves rarely stay in one place for more than six months. The latest versions have electronic launchers, incorporate new electronic-age designs, and have microchip technology that can keep many balls in play at once. Balls can now be automatically fed into the machines from trays, allowing the player to play at more than one machine simultaneously. The new machines have reduced the manual skill needed to play and have speeded up the game. These improvements have increased excitement for the players and the profits for the parlors. Pachinko balls cost the customer about 4 yen each, but a large jackpot can pay off as many as ten thousand shiny pachinko balls!

Most players are male salarymen, but the primary customers vary according to the time of day. Housewives play during the day, young people after school, and in the evening hours the parlors are filled with businessmen and shopkeepers. Children are not permitted to play in pachinko parlors, but there are children's versions of pachinko machines in the amusement sections of Japanese department stores.

In 1990, the average male player spent about 3,300 yen (33 U.S. dollars) per visit. Recently, the average per player has apparently increased, perhaps to 24,000 yen (240 U.S. dollars) per visit.

Why Is Pachinko So Popular?

There are a variety of opinions about the continued popularity of pachinko. According to Hiroshi Takeuchi, Chairman of the Board of Directors of the Long-Term Credit Bank's Research Institute, the main reason so many Japanese play pachinko is to release tension. Jason Priestly, editor of *Kansai Time Out*, believes that "in a country where workers advance according to a set pattern and the notion of a 'fast career lane' is almost nonexistent, pachinko offers the illusion of instant prosperity." Some people are attracted to pachinko simply because they enjoy gambling and there are few other gambling options in Japan.

There are also special circumstances in Japan that contribute to the appeal of pachinko. Japanese homes are small, the cities have few parks, and alternative forms of amusement are not cheap. For example, a movie ticket costs about 18 U.S. dollars— even more if you reserve a seat in advance. The price of tickets to concerts, especially by foreign performers, often exceeds 100

U.S. dollars. Eighteen holes of golf can cost between 50 and 400 U.S. dollars. And none of these options offers the chance to get back some of the initial outlay, except perhaps golf. Considering the special circumstances of Japan, pachinko seems like a good entertainment value combined with a chance to hit the jackpot!

A Harmless Game, or a Gambling Machine?

As an amusement game, pachinko seems harmless enough although the parlors are incredibly noisy and filled with cigarette smoke. But the truth is that many, if not most, players play not for amusement but for money.

In principle, casino-type gambling is illegal in Japan. Lotteries and betting on horse racing are legal, and informal betting occurs elsewhere, such as on the golf course. But the Law on Control and Improvement of Amusement Businesses bans pachinko parlor operators from offering cash or negotiable securities as prizes. Instead, pachinko prizes are nonmonetary items, often unappealing things such as pencil leads or lighter flints. Winners of trays of steel pachinko balls, however, are happy to exchange their winnings for these seemingly worthless prizes, because they can then go to another nearby shop, where they "sell" their newly won merchandise. The dealer at that shop, of course, resells the items back to the pachinko parlor for a profit. The lucky or skillful pachinko player legally wins only prizes, but actually he or she is able to walk away with cash. In that guise, pachinko is officially regarded as a form of amusement rather than a form of gambling. But seasoned players know that playing pachinko is not much different from playing a slot machine in Las Vegas.

Experienced pachinko players recognize that the game involves risks, and they adapt themselves accordingly to minimize losses and maximize winnings. They realize that the odds of winning are not the same on all machines. Machines near the windows are often rigged to yield greater chances of winning so

that passersby will be attracted by the loud noise of cascading balls won by players. When the parlors open in the morning, players are already lined up outside, eager to get to the "best" machines. At the opening of a new parlor, machines are usually programmed to yield higher odds of winning. On the other hand, the days when workers receive their pay or semiannual bonuses are considered bad days to play.

Negative Social Consequences

Addiction to pachinko has serious negative social consequences that parallel those of legalized gambling in the United States. Broken homes and neglected children are not uncommon. There are stories (or male fantasies, perhaps) that some female pachinko addicts offer sex to male parlor operators for tips on hot machines.

Pachinko parlors help sustain organized crime in Japan by paying large sums of "protection money" to crime syndicates. Japanese police estimate that the 1,600 pachinko parlors in Tokyo pay more than 30 billion yen (about 300 million U.S. dollars) per year in protection money to gangster organizations.

There have been efforts to legalize pachinko gambling in Japan. The National Police Agency believes that legalization might result in purging organized crime from the industry. But both the Ministry of Justice and the Ministry of Finance have opposed this proposal for legalization of pachinko gambling.

Because pachinko is a cash-oriented business, the pachinko parlor operators are also suspected of engaging in widespread tax evasion. In the early 1990s, Nippon Leisure Card System and Nippon Game Card Company introduced prepaid pachinko cards patterned after the popular prepaid phone cards in denominations of 1,000 yen to 10,000 yen. More than two-thirds of the pachinko parlors now accept these cards. When a card is used, the company that issued the card reimburses the pachinko parlor for the amount spent in the parlor. The introduction of these cards was applauded by the government, which had hoped that it would be easier to monitor the pachinko industry and reduce tax evasion. Instead, it has spawned a new crime—production and distribution of phony pachinko cards. As with prepaid telephone cards, used cards are not returned to their issuers. Enterprising criminals have figured out a way to revive the used cards by transferring magnetic data from unused cards and reselling them, resulting in tens of billions of yen in losses to the authentic card issuers. The crime is particularly difficult to suppress because pachinko parlors profit whether the cards are fake or authentic. Even when a phony card is used, the original issuer is obliged to reimburse the pachinko parlor.

Pachinko as an Export Industry

Japan has begun to export pachinko to other countries, with parlors in Singapore, Korea, Taiwan, and Beijing. With growing numbers of Japanese visitors traveling to Las Vegas, don't be surprised to find pachinko on your next visit to the megacasinos.

6

Why Are the Japanese Obsessed with Luxury Brand-Name Goods?

Kazuo Nishiyama

Japanese tourists abroad are welcomed by shopkeepers because of their notorious free-spending sprees at famous boutiques and duty-free shops. They are more likely to choose a product based on brand recognition than on price. They don't buy just any brand names, but only those that are recognized and valued at home.

Americans watching Japanese tourists shop in New York or Honolulu are often amazed by the Japanese obsession with brand-name luxury goods. At 7:45 A.M. one morning, before any stores were open for business, a young Japanese office lady (OL—a Japanese name for female office workers, the majority of whom are unmarried) stood on the beach in Waikiki holding a Gucci shopping bag in one hand and two duty-free shop bags in the other hand to have her picture taken by her friend. The shopping bags were strategically held so they faced the camera. For her, Hawaii's scenic beauty was only a backdrop for having friends and relatives at home see that she had made purchases at famous-name stores in Honolulu. A recent article in *The Economist* noted that Japanese women account for a mere 2 percent of the population of Asia, but almost half of the sales of French luxury goods in the region. How do you explain such behavior?

39

Historical Reasons

From the time of the Meiji Restoration (1868), Japan began wholesale borrowing of Western culture and institutions in an attempt to catch up with the West. Japan adopted the British form of government, German medicine, French fashion and educational system, and American business know-how and technology. Former high-ranking samurai warriors began wearing Western suits. High-society women wore Western-style dresses with high-heeled shoes and accessories. They held Western-style cocktail parties and even engaged in social dancing. Modernization was equated with Westernization. Meiji government officials even suggested that small Japanese men marry larger Caucasian women to improve the build and height of the Japanese race. They felt that Japanese men were too short and frail compared to robust Western men. These attitudes were known as "Western worship" *(seiyō sūhai)*. After its defeat in World War II, Japan again imported America's industrial technology, educational system, and democratic system of government along with Hollywood movies and popular youth culture.

Both the Meiji Restoration and World War II encouraged the Japanese to place a high value on Western products. Right after the war, goods of any kind were scarce and their quality was poor; people opted for the safety of a famous name. When quality cannot be easily ascertained by consumers, they tend to associate quality with high prices. These attitudes toward "foreign-made goods" *(gaikoku seihin)* persist today, even though made-in-Japan brand-name items are just as good and sometimes superior to Western goods.

Social Custom

Japanese social custom requires exchange of gifts on many occasions (see chapter 4). According to one survey, the average Japanese family receives or gives one gift per week. Although many people don't like the practice, it is considered part of the social custom. Midsummer gifts *(ochūgen)* and year-end gifts *(oseibo)* are customary for the year's two most important occasions for businesspeople to give gifts to valued clients, both to show appreciation and to ask for continued patronage. Friends and relatives also send gifts to each other to enhance social and family relationships. Politicians, government officials, marriage brokers, and teachers also receive gifts from their beneficiaries during these periods. In addition, gifts are exchanged on such occasions as weddings and special birthdays.

Japan is a status-conscious society (see chapter 26). The price and nature of the obligatory gift depend on the relationship between the two parties and their relative status. For special occasions, every gift must be of high quality, from a prestigious store, and, of course, expensive. For example, one hot-house grown Japanese melon at a famous Japanese department store may cost 15,000 yen (150 U.S. dollars), and a bottle of Napoleon cognac may cost 30,000 yen (300 U.S. dollars). A similar, but less perfect melon might cost only 10 to 30 percent as much in a good grocery store. The Japanese rarely buy such expensive items for their own personal consumption.

Japanese tourists buy souvenirs *(omiyage)* whenever they travel. Before leaving on their trips, they usually receive monetary gifts *(senbetsu)* from family members, relatives, and friends and are expected to bring back souvenirs. A honeymooning couple traveling abroad, having received a lot of *senbetsu,* would have a long shopping list of appropriate souvenirs to communicate respect and gratitude. The list might include expensive French perfumes and Italian silk scarves for the mother-in-law and a very special golf putter for the father-in-law. The new husband may buy expensive Italian silk neckties for superiors and co-workers at his workplace to show his gratitude to them for allowing him to take the days off for his honeymoon. His bride, if she works, will have to buy expensive French cosmetics or Italian silk scarves for her co-workers. The Japanese custom of giving *omiyage* in exchange for *senbetsu* makes Japanese travelers big spenders on famous-name goods both at home and abroad.

Demand for luxury brand-name goods is particularly strong among young female office workers. Usually single and living with their parents, they don't pay for housing and food and thus have a lot of money to spend. They use a good part of their wages and semiannual bonuses for overseas shopping trips. These "bachelor royalty" *(dokushin kizoku)* spend money lavishly, much of it on prestigious brand-name goods, because they know that this free spending will likely come to an end either when they get married or after they have children.

Economic Reasons

Throughout most of the post–World War II period, Japan's huge trading companies controlled imports and prices of most foreign goods through exclusive marketing agreements with their manufacturers. The government helped in this by tightly controlling imports. Informal cartels, retail price maintenance agreements, a costly multilayer retail-wholesale distribution system, and tough government restrictions on imports kept foreign goods from penetrating Japanese consumer markets and kept Japanese domestic prices much higher than prices abroad (see chapter 1). The Japanese became obsessed with brand-name goods, particularly foreign goods, because they were difficult to get even after postwar prosperity had resulted in incomes high enough to pay for them. The scarcity and difficulty of obtaining brand-name goods, combined with Japan's history and social customs, make it hardly surprising that foreign brand-name goods command substantial price premiums in Japan over comparable domestically produced goods.

Signs of Change

The bursting of Japan's "bubble economy" after 1990 has finally injected some practical sense and price-consciousness into Japanese shopping habits. The Japanese are now becoming satisfied with "good-enough" quality products instead of buying only the "best-quality" products. Deregulation in Japan's retail industry, liberalization of import regulations, more vigorous enforcement of the country's Anti-Monopoly Law, break up of retail price-maintenance agreements, and the rising international exchange value of the yen recently have encouraged rapid expansion of discount retailing and have increased imports, promoted competition, and lowered prices (see chapter 7). As famous foreign-brand goods become cheaper and more common in Japan, and as Japan's population ages, making for a rapid decrease in the number of young office ladies, the Japanese obsession with famous foreign-brand goods may soon decline.

There is evidence that this decline may have already begun. Recent surveys by the Japan Travel Bureau have revealed sharp declines since the late 1980s in per-person shopping of Japanese tourists abroad, leading some observers to suggest that the Japanese may have finally satisfied their need for brand-name luxury goods. But for certain goods, particularly those that are given as gifts, Japanese consumers still prefer famous brand-name goods. Hence, the Japanese obsession for brand-name luxury goods is not likely to end soon.

7

Why Are There So Many Small Shops in Japan?

James Mak and Shyam Sunder

Strolling around Motomachi in Kobe and along Shinsaibashi-suji in Osaka or near Kawaramachi dori in the historic Imperial capital of Kyoto, a visitor to Japan is impressed by the large number of small specialty shops and restaurants that line the streets. Surely, Japan must be a nation of small shopkeepers.

Despite the country's high prices, one of the most enjoyable activities for visitors to Japan is shopping, or at least "window shopping." The Japanese also love shopping. On any Sunday in any of Japan's cities, you can barely make your way through the throngs of people on its "shopping streets." Best not be in a hurry to get anywhere!

Shops are not only found in shopping streets and arcades in city centers; they are everywhere. You can buy most daily necessities within a short distance from home. Most of the shops are small, and many are mom-and-pop operated, located in small spaces on the ground floor of the owners' private residence. When a visitor, having bought a bag of Japanese rice, wanted to know the appropriate amount of water to cook it in, the middle-aged shopkeeper went upstairs to get the answer from his wife.

45

Compared to the United States, Japan has over twice as many retail stores per thousand population and Japanese shops average about one-third as many employees and annual sales. In 1994, over half the retail stores in Japan had only one or two employees and over three-quarters of them had less than five employees. Individual ownership accounted for 61 percent of the country's retail stores, but those stores accounted for only 16 percent of total retail sales.

Japan has many large multistory department stores. In recent years, big discount chain stores have begun to proliferate. Large stores that combine a supermarket and a general merchandise department store have emerged under the moniker of "superstores."

Growing even more rapidly are the modern, efficient convenience stores (known as *konbini*), like 7-Eleven. These new, brightly lit stores employ state-of-the art computer technology for monitoring instantaneously the point of sale of each item in each store in order to determine what needs to be restocked. With such sophisticated equipment, the stores can operate efficiently even with relatively untrained, temporary, and part-time workers. Though small in terms of space, the convenience stores enjoy a high volume of business, selling a surprisingly large assortment of goods as well as services, such as payment of utility bills, photocopying, parcel delivery, discount theater tickets, and even travel reservations. The versatility of the convenience stores, along with a twenty-four hour operating schedule, is pushing large numbers of mom-and-pop stores out of business. They are also taking business away from large department stores.

Why Small Stores?

Compared to the United States, Japan has many more small food stores in relationship to its population. In part, this is because Japanese homes are smaller with limited storage, necessitating more frequent visits to stores for buying in smaller quantities. Fresh food, primarily fish and vegetables, which are especially important constituents of the Japanese diet, also call for frequent purchasing. On average, a housewife in Japan visits a food store five times per week, compared to 1.8 times in the United States.

In the United States, better highways and a higher rate of private car ownership encourage the development of suburban malls and large discount stores along highways in areas of low population density. By contrast, the Japanese rely heavily on public transportation and walking, and so stores are built near train and subway stations and in higher-density residential neighborhoods within walking (or biking) distance from private homes and apartment complexes. Having large numbers of people living nearby also makes it easier for small stores to be profitable in Japan. Small stores are popular because they are easily accessible, provide a high level of personal service and offer easier return policies for defective goods. It is not surprising that Japan's retail industry is dominated by large numbers of small shops.

As for the small mom-and-pop stores, they require modest amounts of start-up capital and employ a large number of retirees. Their employment function is particularly important for Japan because social security benefits, until recently, have been less generous than in other industrialized countries. Moreover, retirement age is low in Japan (see chapter 26), while longevity is high.

The Large-Scale Retail Store Law

Although conflict between large and small stores exists in other countries, small shopowners in Japan have been protected by legislation. Large stores threaten the existence of small stores because they are less costly to operate per unit of sale and thus are able to charge lower prices. Small store owners, however, constitute a large political interest group in Japan. In 1947, under political pressure from this group of small shopowners, the government passed the first Department Store Law. That law required permission from the Ministry of International Trade and Industry (MITI) before the opening of a department store or a branch store, or even before increasing existing store space. Nonetheless, fueled by the postwar economic boom, the number of department stores rose sharply in spite of the law. Supermarkets, a new type of large retail store that emerged in the 1960s and 1970s, were not subject to the regulations of the Department Store Law.

To amend the earlier law and to expand its coverage, the government passed the Large-Scale Retail Store Law in 1973. It regulated stores larger than 1,500 square meters (16,145 square feet) of retail space. In Tokyo and eleven other larger cities, this law covered stores bigger than 3,000 square meters. This new law did not reduce the level of conflict between large and small stores, however, and so it was amended again to become applicable to stores with retail spaces in excess of 500 square meters (5,382 square feet). Anyone who wishes to build a store larger than 500 square meters must obtain the consent of the neighborhood retailers. The amended law granted small and medium retail store owners virtual veto power over construction of large new stores in their markets. The law also regulated large stores' business hours, holidays, and sales space.

The Large-Scale Retail Store Law did not totally prevent large stores from opening, but in many cases the law increased the time and cost involved in opening a large, new retail store. The delays resulting from the need to complete legal procedures before opening typically averaged thirty-four months, but in some cases extended to ten years.

The new Large-Scale Retail Store Law also did not totally protect individual small retailers from the large retailers. The number of small retailers reached a peak in the 1980s and has declined steadily since then. Part of the explanation is that the children and grandchildren of many shopkeepers have no interest in taking over the family store. Also, the increase in personal ownership of automobiles has heightened consumer mobility and has expanded the geographical area from which a larger store can draw its retail customers.

The overall economic effects of the law are predictable and, in fact, consumer prices were higher than they otherwise would be in an open competitive retail environment. Also, U.S. and other foreign governments have criticized the law for functioning as an entry barrier to foreign companies trying to enter the Japanese retail sector. In response to such problems, the 1989 Structural Impediments Initiative discussions between the United States and Japan brought about Japan's agreement to begin deregulating the country's distribution system, starting with the Large-Scale Retail Store Law.

Reform of the Large-Scale Retail Store Law

Reform of the Large-Scale Retail Store Law began in 1991 with the passage of a new amendment that changed the review and application processes. Since then, the average amount of time needed for processing an application has been eight months. Moreover, any store or store expansion devoted exclusively to the sale of imported goods does not have to gain the approval of other retailers in the area. Additionally, since May 1994, any store under 1,000 square meters (10,764 square feet) is exempt from the restrictions of the law. Finally, the mandatory closing time for large stores has been extended from 7 P.M. to 8 P.M.

Retail industry deregulation, combined with increasing price sensitivity of Japanese consumers due to the burst of the bubble economy in the early 1990s, have spurred the growth of discount retailing. Huge discount stores, such as Daiei, not only enjoy lower costs because of their large size; they also have enough economic clout to bypass the traditional layers of middlemen in Japan's distribution chain, they can import lower-priced foreign goods, and they can use their growing market power to defy domestic manufacturers' efforts to enforce manufacturers' suggested retail prices. The result is falling prices for the consumer. A can of Coca-Cola, for example, sells for 110 yen in vending machines and 80 to 90 yen in grocery stores. However, Daiei imports a generic cola drink from the United States emblazoned with "Made in America" in big letters and sells it at the introductory price of 39 yen. Gradually, the generic cola is beginning to grab market share.

Reform of the Large-Scale Retail Store Law has also accelerated the entry of foreign retailers into Japan. Toys "Я" Us is often held up as a symbol of a successful foreign retail business in Japan. Since opening its first store in Japan in 1991, Toys "Я" Us rapidly grew to thirty-six outlets in 1995, and plans to have one hundred outlets by the year 2000.

Finally, American-style megamalls are coming to Japan. A partnership of U.S. and Japanese investors recently announced plans to develop four American-style retail-entertainment megamalls in Tokyo and Osaka. The malls will contain U.S. and Japanese retail stores, movie theaters, international cuisine, fitness clubs, and indoor rock-climbing and roller-skating rinks. The partners plan to build ten to twenty malls in Japan in the next decade.

The Landscape of the Future

Deregulation is beginning to transform the retail industry in Japan. For once, in a country where government policies too often have favored producers over consumers, consumers finally seem to have won a round. But with large discount chain stores, foreign retail stores, modern convenience stores, and American-style megamalls sprouting up all over the country, Japan's touristic landscape will no longer be as fascinating to foreign visitors.

8

How Do the Japanese and Americans Spend Their Money?

James Mak

Japanese and American households use their incomes very differently in terms of amounts of savings and ways to spend money.

First, Japanese households save a larger percentage of their after-tax incomes than American households do—14.7 percent versus 4.2 percent, respectively (see chapter 16). Americans might find those numbers hard to believe if they've ever seen Japanese tourists in the United States buying up Gucci bags, Calvin Klein jeans, and everything in sight with famous, and usually European, brand names (see chapter 6). These tourists also shop in stores most Americans would feel too intimidated even to walk into.

As for the income that they spend, American and Japanese households differ in several important categories. To make it easier to compare the two households, let's first look at the numbers in the table on page 52.

These numbers show that the Japanese tend to allocate a much larger share of their budget on food and housing than Americans do, while Americans spend disproportionately more than the Japanese on medical care, transportation, and unspecified "other" expenditures.

Category of Spending	United States	Japan
Food, beverage, and tobacco	10.8%	19.7%
Clothing and shoes	5.8	5.7
Housing	19.0	26.4
Medical care and health expenses	17.5	11.1
Transportation and communications	13.2	9.6
Education, cultural services, and entertainment	10.5	10.6
Other	23.2	16.1

Why do the Japanese spend more of their budget than Americans on food and housing? The answer is simply that food and housing are much more expensive in Japan than in the United States.

High Food Prices

In a land-scarce country like Japan, food is expensive to produce. But it is difficult to imagine that scarcity of land explains why a twenty-two-pound bag of rice at the Daiei discount store in Kobe, Japan, recently sold for 53 U.S. dollars (at an exchange rate of 100 yen to the U.S. dollar), or more than 7 times the price of California medium-grain rice sold at the Daiei store in Honolulu. If land scarcity were the only reason for high food prices, Japan could lower its domestic food prices simply by importing cheap food from land-abundant countries like the United States, Canada, and Australia.

Food prices are high in Japan largely because of Japanese government agricultural policy and regulations. In the past, Japan's powerful agricultural lobby effectively blocked the massive importation of cheap food into the country, and the result has been very expensive food. For instance, rice for consumption as a staple could not be imported into Japan without government permission (see chapter 20). And permission was not granted (period!) except under extraordinary conditions, as in the case of a very poor rice harvest in 1994. Indeed, a few years ago, the Japanese government would not allow California rice growers even to give out free samples at an international fair in Japan.

One reason for the strength of the agricultural lobby in Japan is that election districts were not redrawn until recently despite massive migration of the population from rural to urban areas after World War II. As a result, rural voters came to have far more political power (per capita) than urban voters.

Prospects for lower food prices in the future are improving. Political pressure from the United States and Japan's other trading partners has begun to open up Japan's markets for agricultural imports. Under the recently completed Uruguay Round of General Agreement on Tariffs and Trade (GATT) discussions, Japan has finally agreed to import small amounts of

Bon appetit

Japan is increasingly dependent on food imports.
Here is the percentage of total food consumed in Japan, measured in calorie units, that is produced domestically.

Sources: Asahi Shimbun, *Japan Almanac,* 1997
and *Nikkei Weekly,* April 14, 1997.

rice annually beginning in 1995 (see chapter 20). In the past, liberalization of food imports, such as beef and oranges, has brought down prices in Japan.

High Cost of Housing

Housing, another basic necessity, is also much more expensive in Japan than in the United States. To a visiting foreigner, renting an apartment in Japan can be quite a nerve-rattling experience. First, the rent is exorbitant, at least by American standards. A sample of recent Tokyo rental ads appearing in an English-language newspaper illustrate this point:

Shibuya: one bedroom + living + dining, kitchen, walk to subway and JR rail station, 180,000 yen (or, 1,800 U.S. dollars per month).
Akasaka: Pleasant view, free parking, three bedrooms, good location, 650,000 yen (or, 6,500 U.S. dollars per month).
Meguro: two-bedroom house, spacious, air-conditioned living room, wooden floor, five years old, 350,000 yen (or, 3,500 U.S. dollars per month).

In addition to the astounding rent, it is probable that the renter will also have to pay nonrefundable "key money" *(reikin)* equal to several months' rent. Key money is simply a lump-sum up-front payment to the landlord for the privilege of renting the apartment. It is a practice that is observed in housing markets where there is a severe housing shortage, like where there is strict government rent control. (In Tokyo, where there are presently large numbers of vacant apartment units for foreigners, it is not uncommon to see real estate ads that advertise "no key money" for some units.) In addition to the key money, the renter must also put down a sizable rental deposit *(shikikin)*, which is refundable at the time the apartment is vacated, after subtracting expenditures for any required repairs. The size of the deposit and key money varies from region to region. In the Kansai (Kyoto-Osaka-Kobe) area, the combined key money and deposit (called *hoshōkin*) is much higher than in other regions. Tenants receive no interest on these deposits.

The rents quoted here are for apartments that are intended for foreigners and therefore generally of higher quality and more expensive than what the average Japanese family might pay. Also, rents in Tokyo are much higher than in the rest of the country. A Japanese realtor friend of mine from Kobe told me that a typical young married couple renting a 50-square-meter "2LDK" apartment (that's two small rooms plus a combination living-dining-kitchen area) in an apartment building constructed of concrete would pay around 120,000 yen (or, 1,200 U.S. dollars) per month for rent. The husband, probably a beginning salaryman, would typically earn about 180,000 yen per month (after taxes and excluding the two semiannual bonuses, which can add up to about 4 months' salary). The wife, working part-time, would earn about 50,000 yen for a combined income of 230,000 yen (2,300 U.S. dollars per month). Thus, the rent alone for that typical couple would take up more than half of their combined regular monthly take-home salaries. If they started out in an old wooden building instead, the monthly rent would be about 70,000 yen per month.

Owning a home in Japan is financially out of reach for most young people unless they inherit one. The latest survey conducted by the National Land Agency showed that in 1994 an existing house in the heart of Tokyo (with land) costs about 13 times the average annual Japanese income, and in Osaka, 9.5 times the average income. In contrast, a New Yorker has to pay the equivalent of only 3 times his or her average annual income to buy a house. Not surprisingly, unmarried men and women in Japan usually live with their parents if they are living in the same town or city. It's also not unusual to find several generations of a family living in the same household, called "megahouseholds."

Condominium units are cheaper. Still, the National Land Agency noted that condo prices averaged 5.6 times the buyers' average annual incomes in 1994 (though down from the 8.5 times average annual incomes during the "bubble economy" of the late 1980s).

The high price of land is the main reason for high housing prices in Japan. The National Land Agency survey showed that in 1994, a square meter of residential land in Tokyo averaged 560,000 yen or 5,490 U.S. dollars at the 1994 average exchange rate of 102 yen to the dollar, making Tokyo the most expensive city in the world. By comparison, it was $169 in Los Angeles, $202 in San Francisco, and $485 in Honolulu. Even Hong Kong, the next most expensive city, at $3,500, and Seoul at $1,904 per square meter, pale in comparison to Tokyo when it comes to the price of land. Of course, land prices in Tokyo are much higher than in other areas of Japan, but they have been falling rapidly since the early 1990s.

Because of the high price of land, people in Japan are even thinking of adopting a practice Hawaii is presently discarding—land leasing—as a way to reduce the cost of home ownership. In land leasing, you own the house but rent the land, like in a trailer park. High housing prices have also induced parents and adult children living together to jointly purchase a house by means of a "multigeneration" mortgage. But unlike in the United States, mortgage interest payments (and local property taxes) are not deductible on Japanese income tax returns, making housing even more expensive in Japan.

That housing, both rental and owned, would be expensive in Japan is hardly surprising, considering that land is a scarce commodity in the island nation. But that's not the only reason. Government protection of the agricultural industry and lower taxation of farmland in Japan means that the farm sector is larger than it would be otherwise, and that also means that there is less land available for housing. In a nutshell (or, rice kernel?), land scarcity combined with the government's protectionist policy on agriculture not only explains high food prices; it also helps explain high housing prices in Japan.

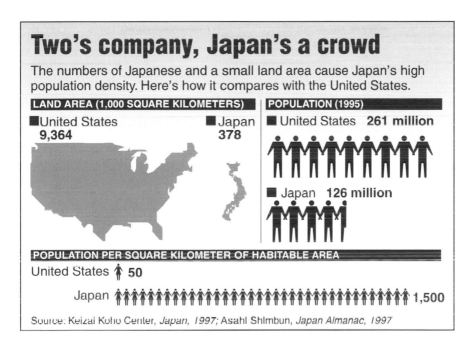

Two's company, Japan's a crowd

The numbers of Japanese and a small land area cause Japan's high population density. Here's how it compares with the United States.

LAND AREA (1,000 SQUARE KILOMETERS)

■United States
9,364

■Japan
378

POPULATION (1995)

■ United States **261 million**

■ Japan **126 million**

POPULATION PER SQUARE KILOMETER OF HABITABLE AREA

United States 🯅 **50**

Japan 🯅🯅🯅🯅🯅🯅🯅🯅🯅🯅🯅🯅🯅🯅🯅🯅🯅🯅🯅🯅🯅🯅🯅🯅🯅🯅🯅🯅🯅🯅 **1,500**

Source: Keizai Koho Center, *Japan, 1997*; Asahi Shimbun, *Japan Almanac, 1997*

Since the Japanese spend larger shares of their budgets on food and housing, it means that they must be spending smaller shares of their budgets on other things.

Less on Health Care and Transportation

Japanese households spend proportionately less of their budgets on health care. That's because, unlike in the United States, the Japanese have universal social health insurance plans that pay most of their medical bills so that their out-of-pocket spending on medical care is much lower than in the United States. The Japanese government also has kept tight control over prices, quality, and scope of health care services. One consequence is that total health care spending per person is also far lower in Japan than in the United States—1,495 U.S. dollars per person versus 3,299 U.S. dollars, respectively (see chapter 21).

The Japanese also spend less on personal transportation. That's because, living in a densely packed country, the Japanese rely much more heavily on their efficient public transit system (trains and buses) than do Americans, who rely more on their (more expensive) personal automobiles. The United States has one passenger automobile for every 1.8 people, compared to one automobile for every three people in Japan.

Who lives better, the Japanese or the Americans? Best read chapter 1 for one person's answer to that question.

9

How Can the Japanese Manage without Personal Checking Accounts?

Toshiki Jinushi and James Mak

In Japan, don't expect to pay your bills by check. There are no personal checking accounts! Businesses can have checking accounts, but not individuals (except for a few very wealthy individuals). You'll have to find some other way to pay for your purchases. What if you want to pay for a magazine subscription? One option is to go to any of the 24,500 post offices (which, by the way, are not open on Saturdays) and instruct the postal service to pay the magazine publisher's account at the postal service. Of course, you have to pay the magazine subscription price plus a service fee to the post office. You can also send cash by registered mail. Utility bills can be conveniently paid at any of the twenty-four-hour convenience stores with no extra service charge. Or you can go to a bank.

Bank Accounts

At the bank, you can fill out a form and give it, and your money, to a teller, and pay each bill in that way. Or, if you have an account, you can arrange with your bank to transfer money electronically from your account to pay some bills. Oh yes, people do have bank accounts. But the bank's service fee for paying bills is higher than that of the postal service. Yet a personal bank account is now necessary in Japan because that's how employers pay their employees, electronically transferring money on pay day. In the past (and still true for some people) employees were usually paid in cash. But electronic transfers are common now. Nevertheless, you can't just stay at home and write checks against your bank account. Before the widespread use of bank transfers, landlords and utility companies usually sent employees door to door to collect money. So there was a time when you could pay your bills without leaving home, but you didn't pay them by writing checks.

The problem with paying bills directly at the bank is that you have to make a separate trip to the bank each time you want to pay a bill. It usually means taking off from work early, since banks close at 3 P.M. on weekdays and are not open on Saturdays. (The post office gives you a bit longer on weekdays.) The only people who can go to the bank during regular banking hours are housewives, retired people, and working people with flexible schedules or with work schedules that just happen to match regular banking hours. There are typically very few men in business suits waiting at teller windows to pay their personal bills. Life in Japan without personal checking accounts can be inconvenient if you're a single salaryman living on your own or a short-term resident.

A Cash Society

Instead of carrying checkbooks, the Japanese tend to carry large amounts of cash with them at all times. While America began to adopt checks as a popular means of paying bills after the Civil War, Japan remains a cash-oriented society. Japan has large numbers of bank automatic teller machines (ATMs)—

one for about every thousand people (see chapter 19). The ATMs are so sophisticated that they allow you to withdraw as little as a 10 yen coin (or 10 U.S. cents) or several million yen in a day. But the machines close at 7 P.M. on weekdays, and when many workers are just getting off work—between 6 and 7 P.M.— the machines charge a fee (103 yen) for usage. There is always a fee if you use an ATM that doesn't belong to your bank. ATMs, which are available for very limited hours on weekends, also can be used to pay some bills, but many people—especially senior citizens—are either intimidated or frustrated by the complicated procedures required to pay bills using ATMs and so prefer to wait in line at the bank. Foreigners may have difficulty using the ATM machines because the operating instructions are in Japanese. In any case, bill payment by ATMs is a relatively recent innovation in Japan, but it is not available on all ATMs, and not for all hours that ATMs operate.

Because there are no personal checks, it is difficult to withdraw money from a Japanese bank account if you are living in the United States. Certainly, you can't simply write a check to withdraw money or to pay for a Japanese book or magazine. The easiest way to get your money out of the bank may be simply to travel to Japan.

In Japan, credit cards were hard to obtain until recently. They are gaining popularity (in 1994, each adult had an average of 2.1 cards), and are used even for buying groceries, but they are still not as widely used as in the United States. In Japan, quite in contrast with the United States, credit cards do not have the prestige of cash. Paying for your dinner by credit card may leave your date wondering if you are using plastic because you have no money except what you borrow.

Why No Personal Checking Accounts?

The most common explanation for the absence of personal checking accounts is "We don't need them." However, that explanation rings hollow for those who are currently making trips to the bank, the post office, or convenience stores or are using other less convenient forms of bill payment and incurring high costs of transacting personal business. Those costs of cash transactions would be even higher were Japan not a low-crime country.

Japan's low crime rates no doubt explain—at least in part— why the Japanese have less need (or demand) for personal checking accounts. The Japanese can carry around large wads of cash or send cash through the mail in relative safety. Whereas Americans might use checks or credit cards to pay for high-priced purchases, the Japanese are likely to pay for the same purchases in cash, even though their largest bill is a 10,000-yen note, about the equivalent of 100 U.S. dollars. Imagine paying for a new car with a stack of bills several inches thick!

The dominance of cash transactions is often explained as a cultural tradition. For the tradition-conscious Japanese, history can be a powerful force against change. Nonetheless, Japanese consumers have shown that they are willing to adopt new forms of payment when the potential benefits of change outweigh the costs. For instance, Japanese tourists visiting Hawaii in the 1970s used to carry large bundles of cash (U.S. currency) with them and quickly became favorite targets of local burglars and robbers. Now, Japanese tourists carry travelers' checks and credit cards. At home, the Japanese are rapidly taking to credit-card purchases (and triggering an epidemic of credit-card bankruptcies).

Absence of a long history of commercial banking is yet another explanation for the absence of personal checking accounts in Japan. According to this theory, Japan hasn't had enough experience with commercial banking for checking accounts to have evolved. But this fails to explain why businesses and some wealthy individuals have checking accounts. Some have suggested that banks in Japan were always intended to serve businesses, not consumers. But that fails to explain why Japanese commercial banks, after some initial reluctance, now

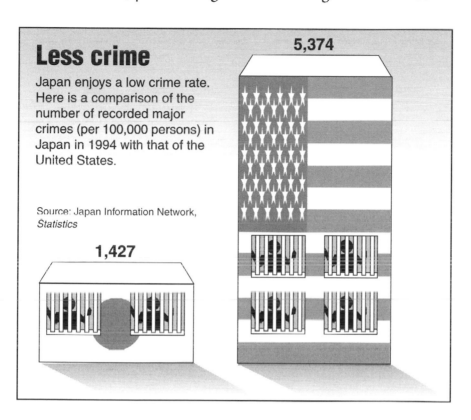

Less crime

Japan enjoys a low crime rate. Here is a comparison of the number of recorded major crimes (per 100,000 persons) in Japan in 1994 with that of the United States.

Source: Japan Information Network, *Statistics*

5,374

1,427

issue consumer credit cards in order to compete with credit card companies and retail merchants.

Yet another potential explanation is the technological leap-frog theory. This theory says that a latecomer to banking, like Japan, may leap-frog over an old technology (like checking accounts) when superior and lower-cost technology alternatives (like credit cards and electronic banking and bill payment) come along. For instance, U.S. banks are offering home-computer banking accounts. Citibank of New York has an ad saying, "No checks, no stamps, no envelopes." Of course, you have to have a home computer and software. In home-computer banking, customers still receive their bills in the mail, but they pay by electronic fund transfer. Some U.S. companies are now offering

CheckFree E-Bill service, which enables customers to receive bills and to pay them electronically.

The technological leap-frog theory won't hold enough water for even a small splash: personal checking accounts continue to be widely used in the United States despite the introduction of credit cards and electronic banking and bill-paying. In 1995, 80 percent of all noncash transactions in the United States were made by check. Electronic payment is clearly not displacing the use of checks. In fact, between 1987 and 1993, payments by check grew faster than electronic payments.

Some people surmise that businesses in Japan would resist personal checking accounts because personal signatures are too easily forged. Signatures are generally not accepted on contracts in Japan or when you open a bank account, unless you're a foreigner. You must use a personal chop *(hanko)*, and for some transactions, such as purchasing a medium- or large-sized car, you must use a *hanko* that has been registered with the government office of the city where you live. On the other hand, merchants in Japan accept, and indeed generally require, a signature on the charge slip when you charge a purchase to your credit card.

For businesses, there are several benefits of not having to accept checks. In Japan, no late bill-payer can use the excuse, "The check's in the mail." There are no bounced checks either, so they don't have to subscribe to check verification services, bother with costly debt collection services, or write off bad checks. Yet the credit card example illustrates that Japanese merchants can adapt to new payment arrangements when competition forces them to do so.

No Checks May Be in the Interest of the Banks and the Post Office

None of the explanations given so far examines the interests of commercial banks in Japan. Banks like electronic banking be-

IF JAPANESE BANKS SERVED ICE CREAM

cause they save on check-processing costs. Nonetheless, even if they prefer not to be in the personal checking account business, you would think that competition would force them to offer checking accounts to people who demand them. An anecdotal piece of evidence suggests that the potential demand for personal checking accounts may be sizable. When one of us went to his bank branch at 2 P.M. to pay his apartment rent, the number issued to him in the queue to pay bills was 432; there were thirty-four people ahead of him! It took one hour and ten minutes, including travel time, to complete the transaction.

Introduction of personal checking accounts could hurt the government's Postal Savings Office (PSO) even more than the commercial banks (see chapter 22). The PSO currently offers the lowest-cost money transfer service in Japan. If there were personal checks, many people would no longer have to go to the post office to transfer money to pay their bills but could instead simply write checks against their bank checking accounts.

Absence of personal checking accounts suggests that there might be at least an implicit agreement among the half dozen or so large banks in Japan not to engage in new competition that might be destabilizing to the cozy relationship that characterizes Japan's banking industry. As in the case of limited ATM hours (see chapter 19), such implicit agreements in Japan seem to be arrived at and maintained with the active support of the government.

Absence of personal checking accounts is often used as yet another piece of evidence by critics of the Japanese system who believe that the system favors producers over consumers.

10

What Are Most
Japanese Doing
on Tax Day?

Robert K. McCleery

Answer: Definitely *not* working on their tax returns.

Each year the Internal Revenue Service (IRS) sends out nearly 8 billion pages of forms and instructions to nearly 100 million American taxpayers. If placed end to end, those pages would circle the Earth nearly twenty-eight times.

What do Americans hate most about meeting the April 15 deadline for filing their personal income tax returns? For most people, it's the stress that comes from having to sort out and work through piles of disorganized receipts (if you can find them!), reading incomprehensible instructions and forms, and struggling with distasteful math. A recent estimate sets the minimum value of the total time individuals spent on their federal tax returns in 1993 at a staggering $50 billion. The stress in filing your annual returns is compounded if you find that you owe the IRS still more money, or even worse, penalty and interest. Some people procrastinate and postpone the unavoidable by filing for extensions. No wonder many Americans are attracted to the idea of a "flat tax," which promises to simplify the tax code, allowing them to file their annual federal tax returns on a form the size of a postcard. Or, for some people, perhaps not to file a return at all. Hallelujah!

What about Japan? It is said that there are only two things you can't escape: death and taxes. How have the Japanese managed to escape from doing their personal income taxes?

Japanese Tax Day

As my first income tax day in Japan rolled around, I was apprehensive about having to go through the same ordeal in Japan, and in Japanese. Knowing the Japanese penchant for rules and regulations, I was convinced that the ordeal would be far worse than in the United States. When the dreaded due-date for taxes approached, I got a phone call from a university accountant. "Excuse me, Dr. McCleery, we need to talk to you about your taxes." (Groan! I thought to myself.) "Did you or your wife have any additional income outside your university salary?" "No?" "Thank you very much." Wait! Don't I have to fill out twenty pages of forms in Japanese? Aren't there two or three similar versions of tax forms, like federal, state, and local income taxes, that I have to file? "No, that's all the information we need. Thank you," replied the accountant. That was it. I had nothing to do with the dreaded Tax Man. What was withheld from my monthly paychecks was all that I owed. There was a simple year-end reconciliation, but that, too, was handled by the university accounting office.

Why Is It So Easy?

Unlike the United States, which requires individuals to self-assess their incomes and then file tax returns with the IRS, Japan uses the withholding system. In Japan, employers and payers of income are required by the government to withhold part of each worker's income and to remit that amount to the government on behalf of each taxpayer. The incomes subject to withholding include wages and salaries, retirement income, interest and dividends, and capital gain from the sale of stocks. Therefore, for most people their employers are their tax collectors, and they are also the ones who do the paperwork. Most Japanese never have to deal directly with government tax officials because withholding rates are calibrated to take into account differences in tax rates for different income levels and for different types of income—progressive rates apply to employment and retirement income, a 20 percent fixed rate is applied to interest and capital gains, and a 35 percent rate is uniformly applied to dividend income. The rates also account for allowable exemptions and deductions. In 1991, 73.6 percent of individual taxpayers in Japan paid their taxes only through withholding of wages and salaries; another 12 percent who had interest, dividend income, and capital gains from the sale of stocks also paid their taxes through withholding and did not have to file a final return.

The Japanese tax system does require some individuals to assess their own income and to pay their own taxes by filing individual tax returns. These include self-employed persons, farmers, and those who receive capital gains from the sale of valuable items such as paintings, jewelry, and real estate. But these persons represent less than 5 percent of all taxpayers.

Withholding provides advantages for both taxpayers and the government. For taxpayers, it eliminates stress and effort. For the government, it reduces tax evasion, since withholding makes it very difficult for a waged or salaried worker to underreport income or to avoid paying taxes. Withholding also reduces the cost of tax collection to the government. Instead of having to deal directly with 47 million individual taxpayers, the tax bureau only has to deal with 3.5 million withholding agents.

But Is It Fair?

Simplicity can be a virtue, but is the Japanese tax collection system fair to all taxpayers?

In Japan, fringe benefits are either not taxed or only partially taxed. This is also true of some company-provided fringe benefits in the United States, such as company contributions to employee retirement funds and health plans. In Japan, the most important company-provided benefit is the value of subsidized housing. Many Japanese employees, particularly those who work for large companies or the government, receive a housing subsidy or company housing, and these benefits are not taxed. Employees of large companies also benefit from cheap or free use of company-provided recreational facilities and additional benefits that are excluded from taxable income. On top of that, many business executives are given generous expense accounts for taking guests out to play golf, to eat at expensive restaurants, and to drink at after-hour hostess bars. These benefits, too, are excluded from taxable income. The exclusion of these many fringe benefits from taxable income clearly introduces inequity into the Japanese income tax system, particularly to the benefit of workers employed by large companies (see chapter 12).

There is also widespread belief, especially among waged and salaried workers, that the tax collection system is unfair because self-employed persons and farmers, who assess their own incomes and pay tax authorities directly, can avoid and evade taxes (see chapter 20). The percentages 9-6-4 are often used to describe the unfair tax system. That means 90 percent of the income of waged and salaried workers is identified and taxed by the authorities, 60 percent of the income of self-employed persons (including doctors and lawyers), and only 40 percent of the income of farmers.

I don't know if these percentages are accurate, but with less than 5 percent of the taxpayers falling in that privileged group, I am inclined not to quibble over this inequity of the Japanese tax system. Moreover, the passage of a national consumption (i.e., sales) tax in 1989 has made it harder for self-employed individuals and farmers to avoid paying taxes. For myself, I am simply ecstatic about not having to fret over the dreaded tax day.

Work

11

Why Do Students Take It Easy at the University?

Shigeyuki Abe, Shoji Nishijima,
Shyam Sunder, and Karen Lupardus

Japan has one of the highest literacy
rates in the world. Its industrious and educated labor force accounts for the high volume, variety, and quality of its industrial products, and are the base of its postwar economic success. Yet most Japanese university students consider their colleges and universities merely as four-year playgrounds. Why?

Japan's Ministry of Education (Monbusho) oversees an egalitarian primary and lower secondary public education system by exercising its broad authority over school curriculum, teaching manuals, and school texts. Admission to coveted schools is determined almost entirely by once-a-year competitive entrance examinations at junior and senior high school levels (see chapter 3). All students must go through "examination hell" to enter the nation's prestigious and well-established hierarchy of public and private universities. About 40 percent of all high school graduates are admitted into some kind of higher education institution. Over 70 percent of the students pursuing postsecondary education are admitted into four-year colleges and universities.

Once admitted, science and engineering students have to study fairly hard to graduate. However, most Japanese university students, especially those enrolled in liberal arts programs, cruise for the next four years. High school students in Japan consider universities as playgrounds that offer them a four-year hiatus between the discipline and rigors of study in lower education and a lifetime of long hours toiling for paternalistic employers after college (see chapters 12 and 13).

Class Attendance

Most Japanese university students do not attend class regularly. In liberal arts and social science classes, daily attendance averages below 20 percent of the class roster. Those who do attend are often more interested in socializing with their classmates than in listening to their instructors. After roll-call, many students sleep in class while others chatter away, oblivious to the lecture. What do students do when not in class? Extracurricular club activities on campus, part-time jobs, travel, volunteer work, and other nonacademic activities take up most of the students' time. A 1995 survey of undergraduate students at Kobe University, a national (public) university, reveals that 59 percent of the students do not study at home, and another 30 percent study no more than an hour per day. Only 31 percent of the students said that they attend classes most of the time; another 37 percent indicated that they attend fairly frequently. In a multiple-response portion of the survey, nonattendance of classes was attributed to boring lectures (65 percent), club activities (26 percent), no intention to study (20 percent), no particular reason (20 percent), and part-time work (12 percent). Ninety-four percent of Kobe University undergraduates hold part-time jobs. In the United States, less than two-thirds of college students hold part-time jobs.

Not surprisingly, university administrators routinely assign classes with large rosters to small classrooms, knowing full well that only a small percentage of the students enrolled are likely to attend. If all registered students showed up, many classrooms would not even have standing room. Although universities rarely limit course enrollment, they are obliged to schedule exams in rooms large enough to accommodate all enrolled students.

The curriculum of Japanese universities is typically divided into two semesters of year-long, lightweight courses, each course usually having one final examination at the end of the year. It is rare for a student to fail these exams. Professors frequently put little effort into their lectures and most give no homework assignments. Easy exams and soft grading curves allow most students to sail through without learning much. In social science and humanities courses, a night of cramming before the examination is usually sufficient to earn a passing grade. Even that is unnecessary if the exam is open book. Seventy-nine percent of all Japanese university students graduate within four years of entering college. It is hardly a demanding or stressful environment for students.

Incentive Structures

The weakness of the Japanese university system can be traced to the incentives of students, professors, and potential employers of graduates (see chapter 12).

From elementary to university level, Japan's educational system screens and selects students for advancement through competition. The annual "entrance examination hell" identifies the best and brightest high school students for admission to the most prestigious universities, such as Tokyo University and Kyoto University. Japanese companies rely on this rigorous screening system to divide the entrants into ability pools. Some companies only hire graduates from specific universities. Admission to select universities virtually guarantees plum jobs. Grades are unimportant to Japanese employers and, therefore, to students. As a spokesman for Sumitomo Bank stated:

> In Japanese colleges, many students spend four years without doing much of anything, so it is a plus for a student if he can say he did something with devotion. . . . We don't require them to submit grades. Even if the grades are bad, it does not necessarily mean that we don't want a student. We stress personal characteristics.

Why, then, do employers not directly hire those who do well on university entrance examinations? Why wait for the students to spend four years in college?

In Japanese organizations, job assignments are often given to groups rather than to individuals. Japanese employers are interested in group and interpersonal skills in their employees, skills that may help raise the productivity of the organization as a whole. From the employer's point of view, the student's participation in extracurricular activities that develop interpersonal skills and build personal relationships among classmates is more important than high grades. But this sounds like a weak rationalization for missing four years of classes and acquiring little substantive knowledge. After all, learning group skills is not incompatible with learning the subject matter.

Japanese companies typically provide new recruits with extensive and intensive in-house training, followed by a succession of job assignments for further on-the-job training. While U.S. firms recruit for specific jobs, Japanese firms discover through successive on-the-job training assignments those jobs that are best suited to the abilities of individual employees. Additionally, lower labor market employee mobility allows the larger Japanese companies to recoup their investment in training new employees. Again, it is unclear why more attention to learning in college will not benefit these companies.

The "Commons" Problem

Basically, Japanese higher education seems to suffer from a "commons" problem in the labor market for students. Merit-based admission to universities results in stratification of universities by the natural abilities of the students they attract. College admission is a highly informative, though imperfect, signal of individual student talent, and this information is available to all employers free of charge. The information content of this signal in Japan is so high that in making their hiring decisions, employers don't consider it worthwhile to make an effort to learn more about the talents of individual job applicants. When most employers find this approach an attractive hiring strategy to follow—like grazing in the commons—the incentives for college students to learn is reduced. If grades are less important to their potential employers than networking, it is hardly surprising that most students care little about studying, class attendance, or grades.

Professors also have little incentive to teach well. If few students care about learning, professors lose interest in teaching. They pursue research or outside income. There is no penalty for teaching poorly. Japanese university professors receive tenure on the date they are hired into a tenurable position, without having to serve the probation period common in American universities. There are no student evaluations of their teaching performance. Professors' salaries and promotions depend on age, length of service, and sometimes research, but not on how well they teach.

Individual employers cannot break out of this vicious cycle of collective indifference because one firm's additional effort to increase screening of students will provide little inducement to all students to learn more during their college years or for professors to improve their teaching. In countries where admission to college is not based on merit alone, college admission is less indicative of talent and merit, and employers find it worthwhile to invest their recruitment effort into investigating individual candidates. This effort provides enough incentive for individual students to strive to learn so they can distinguish themselves in the eyes of potential employers.

The Cost of Education

Tertiary education in Japan is expensive. Annual tuition at national universities averages 336,000 yen (3,360 U.S. dollars) per year. At private universities, the tuition is much higher, averaging about 912,000 yen (9,120 U.S. dollars) per year. In 1992, 6.3 trillion yen (63 billion U.S. dollars) was spent directly on higher education, of which 65 percent came from private funds, 30 percent from national funding, and 5 percent from local governments. To that must be added a large chunk of substantial but difficult-to-measure employee training costs, which could have been avoided if Japanese universities did their job better. The opportunity cost of lost wages while students attend college—estimated at about 2.6 million yen per year for males in 1995—must also be added to the cost of education. There is also the cost of attending cram schools (juku) and special prep schools (yobikō) to prepare for university entrance examinations (see chapter 3). And those who fail the entrance examinations must spend more money on tutoring or attending (*yobikō*) while waiting to take the exams the following year.

Does It Pay?

Does it pay to go to college? The following table compares annual earnings (regular wages plus bonuses) in 1995 of male employees with different educational backgrounds at different ages.

Annual Earnings of Male Employees by Education: 1995
(in 1,000 yen)

Age	High School Graduate	College Graduate
20–24	3,307	3,207
25–29	4,049	4,545
30–34	4,733	5,767
35–39	5,331	6,834
40–44	5,990	7,916
45–49	6,553	9,224
50–54	7,026	10,251
55–59	6,284	9,915
60–64	4,451	7,702

For both groups, lifetime earnings rise with age, reach a peak in the mid-fifties, and decline thereafter. However, college graduates have steeper earning profiles than high school graduates. Between the ages of twenty and twenty-four, a college graduate just beginning a career earns less than a high school graduate with several years of work experience. By his late twenties, however, the college graduate has surpassed the high school graduate in earnings. The gap between their earnings widens rapidly, so that between the ages of fifty and fifty-four, the college graduate earns 46 percent more than the high school graduate. However, not all the observed differences in earnings between the two groups can be attributed to graduation from college. University graduates earn higher incomes partly because, on average, they have more natural ability. There are also nonmonetary benefits to college graduation. As in the United States, Japanese university graduates have higher social status and prestige, get better jobs, have greater chances of promotion, are regarded as more desirable marriage partners, and so on.

Change Is Under Way

Japan's higher education system needs reform. Why don't employers, taxpayers, and students complain about the low-quality education and demand reform? In the post–World War II period, Japan's economy boomed, profits and incomes rose rapidly, resources were abundant, and people did not want to rock the boat. But Japan's economic growth has slowed. The strong yen has induced many Japanese corporations to move their manufacturing plants abroad. Labor shortage has turned into labor surplus, and more employees are being let go during a downturn. As Japan increasingly faces cost pressures from abroad, it will be difficult to continue to sink resources into a costly but low-quality higher education system. The Ministry of Education as well as the universities are under pressure to improve their performance.

Changes are coming to the universities, including (1) the abolition of the current Ministry of Education's "general education" *(kyōyōbu)* core requirements in favor of locally determined programs, (2) the closing of junior colleges, (3) the expansion of graduate programs, (4) the institution of "self-evaluation" by the faculty, (5) the encouragement of student evaluation of faculty, (6) increased emphasis on publication and other evidence of faculty development, (7) encouragement and funding for computerization and development of computer literacy, (8) the abolition of English as a requirement (universities can offer other foreign languages and determine their own foreign language requirements), (9) increased emphasis on international exchange programs, and (10) a recommendation to hire faculty on a fixed-term contract basis.

If these changes are implemented, Japan may finally see meaningful higher education reform.

12

Why Do Japanese Companies Hire Only Spring Graduates?

Teruyuki Higa

New graduates pour forth from Japanese universities in March of each year and officially begin their employment in April. This phenomenon is also the culmination of several months of concentrated, large-scale hiring efforts of Japanese companies and governments. Only the most fortunate, best graduates are hired by the large, well-established companies or enter civil service and enjoy virtual lifetime employment. The less lucky, if they do find a job, are hired by smaller companies that do not have the resources of the larger and governmental employers, and are therefore less likely to find desirable lifetime employment. A few stragglers, usually less than one percent, who graduate in the fall, along with an increasing number of spring graduates will not enter "regular" employment immediately after graduation. These hapless individuals may be destined for a lifetime of intermittent or self-employment. In Japan, anyone who deviates from the normal pattern of moving directly from school to work is regarded as a misfit. At other times of the year, companies usually restrict their hiring to temporary, part-time, or seasonal workers.

This mass, once-a-year hiring routine, known as *shinki gaku-sotsu ikkatsu saiyō* (all-at-one-time hiring of new graduates) I call "shot-gun hiring." It requires close coordination among schools, teachers, job hunters, and employers to screen out and deliver the best graduates to Japan's largest corporations and government bureaucracies. The system of coordinated hiring works so well that it has become a key institutional feature of Japan's post–World War II labor market, along with lifetime employment, compensation based on seniority rather than merit, and enterprise (i.e., company) unionism.

How Does Shot-gun Hiring Work?

Japanese companies agree not to recruit college seniors before the middle of the summer preceding their March graduation. This agreement between Japanese companies and universities has been in place in various forms since 1953, except during the 1962–1973 period. (Some companies do not abide by the hiring agreement, and try to recruit students before the agreed-upon dates. This practice, called *aotagai*, means "to buy up the rice before it is harvested.") Schools and employers agree not to post employment opportunities earlier than July 1, after which time the schools will help their students complete applications and schedule screening tests and interviews. The value and prestige of schools in Japan, as elsewhere, are linked to the performance of their graduates in the labor market. Not surprisingly, schools compete vigorously to place their graduates with better companies; and this is particularly true of private universities, which make up the majority of the colleges and universities in Japan.

Students who pass the initial screening are first granted interviews in groups of a dozen or more. Formal interviews begin around August 1. A select few are offered a second, more personal interview. Because teamwork is so important in Japan's work culture, employers assign a great deal of weight to graduates who were active participants in extracurricular club activities where desirable group cohesion and group competitive skills are developed. Grades are not as important.

Companies are allowed to make job offers after October 1. Those students who are offered jobs commit themselves to work for the company of their choice when they finally graduate in March. The most attractive jobs—usually at the largest corporations, which offer higher salaries, better fringe benefits, more personal privileges, and the potential for valuable connections—are offered to graduates from the most prestigious universities.

Why Hire Inexperienced Graduates?

Marriage is the traditional metaphor for employment in Japan. Both are supposed to imply a lifetime commitment (see chapter 3). Purity and absence of either prior use or preexisting commitments are important in both. Because it is difficult and costly to verify the personal histories of experienced workers, Japanese companies prefer to search for employees among new graduates. Even more important, young recruits are easier to train and mold into obedient and loyal team players. Candidates with prior work experience are more difficult to fit into a company's internal culture. On infrequent occasions when companies are forced to look for specialized skills not available internally, they may hire experienced workers. But even then, these experienced employees may be given special and separate treatment. In a system where workers are paid according to seniority rather than merit, young and inexperienced recruits are also more economical to hire.

Just to make sure that older workers do not slip in under the guise of spring graduates, companies typically place an upper age limit of twenty-four to twenty-five years on candidates who are allowed to take the employment screening tests. In the United States, this practice would be considered age discrimination and thus illegal. But Japan's Constitution and the Labor Standards Law do not bar age discrimination in the labor market at the time of hiring. It is common, even among American companies doing business in Japan, to set age limits in their job announcements. One consequence of the age limit is that it discourages students from taking a year off from school or after graduation to "find themselves," at least not if they aim to climb the corporate or bureaucratic ladder. Another consequence is that you are likely to see only three types of Japanese people who travel abroad: salarymen or company employees traveling on company business, office ladies—who have little hope of career advancement—traveling on their own before they get married, or retired people. Few young Japanese men travel abroad on their own.

Shot-gun Hiring and the Japanese Management System

Seniority-based promotions and wages lie at the root of the Japanese management structure. The managerial hierarchy is built on layers of successive cohorts of entrants of uniform age and education. A steady climb up the corporate ladder is a continuation of the process found in Japanese schools. Many Japanese see this as their system of social and hierarchical control at work and school.

In Japanese companies, promotions come slowly and incrementally. Only after many years of service do a few begin to pull slightly ahead of others in their cohort. Advancement ahead of a senior is less likely, and comes even later in the career. Under this slow pace, any dissatisfaction with the company surfaces late in the career. By that time, the worker has already invested so much of himself into the company that he cannot afford to be too disruptive. In Japan starting salaries are deliberately set low, but rise steeply with seniority (see chapter 14). A worker who is unhappy at work or who gets overlooked for a promotion has to pay a severe financial penalty if he chooses to quit. An employee of a large company will usually work for ten years before taking the risk of changing jobs. And a risk it is: usually the only alternative is to move to a smaller company at a lower salary. Financial loss in terms of lifetime earnings, including lost pension benefits, has been estimated to be large enough to buy a house, something of substantial value in Japan.

Benefits of Shot-gun Hiring

Japanese companies operate in a tightly networked economic system. Larger companies contract out work to progressively smaller companies in the network who have less market power and who often rely on their bigger and more powerful customers for survival (see chapter 25). The larger companies at the top are better paymasters than mid-sized or smaller companies. So, Japanese students, from their youth, strive to advance through a brutally competitive and hierarchical school system in hopes of eventually being hired by one of the "big"—synonymous with "good"—firms (see chapter 3). "Good" firms are not defined solely by their economic size, but also by their history and reputation. A company that does not respect the normal hiring procedure will be seen as overly aggressive or "foreign," and may find itself shut out from getting its share of business in this closed economic network. It may also be shunned by the graduates of the most prestigious universities.

Not surprisingly, most Japanese companies and government bureaucracies follow the established shot-gun hiring routine. By cooperating, they gain access to highly motivated graduates, cooperation and assistance from school career placement services, discounts on travel and training fees (especially important for smaller companies without their own training

divisions), dissemination of job information through employ-
ment-related magazines, and cost-savings from batch processing
a large number of job applicants at one time to select a few employees. Shot-gun hiring also reduces the cost of job search for
students, though it does limit their employment opportunities.
And, of course, from the Japanese employers' point of view,
having everyone begin their contract at the same time simpli-
fies the paperwork.

Can This System Last?

As long as the Japanese economy grew at a furious pace, its
management system and its accouterments of the shot-gun system of hiring, lifetime employment, and seniority wage-promo-
tion were seen as the foundation of success.

But the recent economic slowdown has created new cross-cur-
rents in the system, and has exposed some of the problems. Bet-
ter-paid workers want more leisure time. And the labor shortage
of only a few years ago has now turned into labor surplus and rising unemployment. In 1995, 25,000 new university graduates
(or 7 percent of the total number of graduates) could not find
employment at graduation. Japan's low birth rate has shrunk the
base of its demographic pyramid. And the children of Japan's
baby boomers are now pushing to enter the workforce even
while their parents are being laid off. Higher wages are pushing
domestic manufacturers abroad while foreign companies and
their products have begun to proliferate. Without their own hierarchy of senior people to work with, foreign corporations are
luring away experienced employees from Japanese companies.
They find a ready source among discontented workers and
among a large pool of qualified women who wish to enter and
remain in career employment but continue to face substantial
gender discrimination at Japanese companies (see chapter 26).

Today's changing social, technological, and economic environment calls for a different management structure and

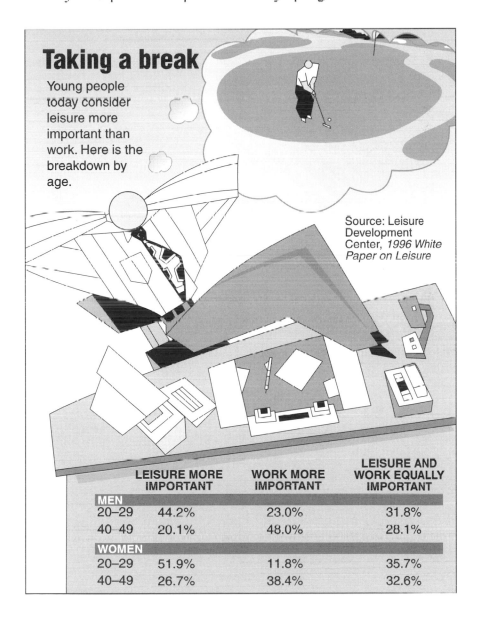

Taking a break

Young people today consider leisure more important than work. Here is the breakdown by age.

Source: Leisure Development Center, *1996 White Paper on Leisure*

	LEISURE MORE IMPORTANT	WORK MORE IMPORTANT	LEISURE AND WORK EQUALLY IMPORTANT
MEN			
20–29	44.2%	23.0%	31.8%
40–49	20.1%	48.0%	28.1%
WOMEN			
20–29	51.9%	11.8%	35.7%
40–49	26.7%	38.4%	32.6%

personnel policy. Japan needs to have a more individually adaptive, creative, technologically advanced, and flexible workforce, which means looking beyond the shot-gun hiring system that served the system reasonably well in the past.

Japanese companies are beginning to adopt more flexible hiring practices. The largest corporations are looking for employees from a broader range of universities and year-round recruiting, and some companies are even looking at workers with prior work experience. More Japanese companies are switching from the system of lifetime employment to one of hiring by contract for fixed-term periods. In the past ten years, the proportion of full-time regular (as opposed to short-term contract) employees in Japanese companies has fallen from 83 percent to 78 percent and continues to fall. Increasingly full-time employees are being replaced by part-time employees.

In recent years, employer groups such as the Japan Federation of Employers' Associations (Nikkeiren) have urged that this collusive hiring agreement between Japanese companies and universities be terminated. The agreement was not renewed for 1997. Small- and medium-sized companies are apprehensive that the end of this agreement will give large corporations even greater competitive advantage in hiring quality employees. Universities complain that uncoordinated recruiting will distract students and disrupt their education, though their unspoken concern is probably the loss of the easy hiring channels for their graduates. But everyone seems to be resigned to the change. Japan led the world in transforming manufacturing from mass to flexible methods. A change from mass to flexible hiring has just begun.

13

Why Don't Workers Claim All Their Overtime?

Teruyuki Higa and Karen Lupardus

Japanese workers have a reputation for working long overtime hours. Curiously, they don't usually ask to be paid for all the extra hours they work. Imagine an employee who leaves the office one night at 11 P.M., six hours after the normal quitting time. Allow an hour for dinner. If the employee claims three hours of overtime, the remaining two hours would be considered "service overtime," or unpaid overtime. Imagine now that it is not just one employee, or an occasional night at the office, but that it is a regular routine for many Japanese workers—two-fifths of them, as indicated in a survey taken at the peak of the bubble economy. With 50 million workers, the total amount of such unpaid overtime in Japan was staggering.

How Much Unpaid Overtime do Japanese Workers Put In?

There are no official statistics on the amount of unpaid overtime. However, it is possible to estimate its magnitude by comparing the hours of work computed by the Ministry of Labor for its Monthly Labor Survey (MLS) with the hours computed by the Management and Coordination Agency for its Labor Force

Survey (LFS). For its estimate, the MLS computes hours of work based on the payrolls of firms that indicate the paid hours of work. That number is smaller than the one estimated by the LFS, which is based on interviews of workers and reports the number of hours they claim to have worked. In 1994, the MLS figure for hours of work averaged nearly 167 hours per month for male workers, while the LFS figure was 47 hours per week (about 204 hours per month). Computed over an entire year, the MLS figures amount to 2,003 hours while the LFS figures show 2,444 hours. In other words, in 1994, the average Japanese male worker gave his company 441 hours of unpaid overtime. Another way of looking at it is that these workers were paid only 82 percent of the hours that they actually worked. The extra unpaid hours don't show up in official international labor statistics when comparing hours of work put in by workers from different countries.

If the hours of work claimed by the Japanese workers are correct, it means that the average male worker was at his job every day of the year except Sundays, putting in eight hours on weekdays and six hours on Saturdays. Contribution of free overtime is especially prevalent among salaried male white-collar managers and salesworkers.

The Economics of Unpaid Overtime

In Japan, Dr. Pepper has begun a campaign of offering 500 milliliter cans for the same price as 350 milliliter cans. When Dr. Pepper offers an extra 150 milliliters of soda apparently for "free," it is actually lowering the price of its product. The same is true of service overtime. By working extra hours for "free," the worker is actually receiving a lower hourly wage than the nominal (i.e., stated) wage because everybody involved expects to and does deliver more hours of work than was agreed to in the nominal contract. That lowers the effective wage rate without lowering the nominal wage rate. Thus, the true labor content per unit of Japanese goods and services produced is actually higher (and the true wage rate is lower) than suggested by official government statistics.

Unpaid overtime increases the flexibility of the Japanese wage structure. During the recent prolonged economic recession, while hours of work reported in Japanese official labor statistics declined, free overtime appears to have remained unchanged and may have even increased. A comparison of data for males in 1992 and 1994 suggests that unpaid overtime may even have increased from 435 hours in 1992 to 441 hours in 1994. Since nominal wages in Japan are negotiated through collective bargaining (see chapter 14), they cannot be unilaterally reduced by employers even during a recession, when the demand for labor is falling. The alternative is to increase the amount of employee unpaid overtime, and in that way companies lower their *effective* wage rates and thus reduce the need to lay off workers.

How Do Companies View Unpaid Overtime?

Japanese companies customarily operate under a labor-shortage environment, resulting in heavy work assignments for each employee. The result is a heavy reliance on overtime. Even when labor is available, companies are cautious about hiring additional regular employees. Operating under the lifetime employment system (see chapter 12), many Japanese companies won't hire new employees when business is good because they can't fire them when business is poor. It should therefore come as no surprise that Japanese companies benefit from unpaid overtime.

From the company's perspective, workers contribute free overtime out of consideration for the welfare of the company or to express their loyalty to the firm. Japanese workers, especially men, often stay late at the office even when they appear not to be doing any work (see chapter 15). They simply don't leave, either because their bosses or their colleagues haven't left for the day, a practice known as "compassionate overtime." They might be reading newspapers or playing video games at their desks. While their staying late doesn't contribute directly to company productivity, they are displaying their loyalty and dedication to the company. They are available in case they are needed. In Japanese companies, dedication and loyalty may be more important than the results of the additional unpaid hours that employees put in at work.

How Do Workers View Unpaid Overtime?

A survey conducted by Sohyo (National Association of Workers' Unions) found that the most common reason workers gave for contributing unpaid overtime was simply, "I like to finish my tasks on a daily basis." From a worker's point of view, work unfinished one day adds to the next day's work. Even worse, it may inconvenience his co-workers or the company's customers or clients.

At the same time, workers recognize that by contributing unpaid overtime to their company, they are also underwriting their own economic security and financial well-being. Their contribution of free overtime could mean larger bonuses next year. It could also mean that their company will not go bankrupt, and they will not have to look for another job. Concern about the company's well-being is very much at the forefront of Japanese workers' thoughts. They know that an experienced employee from a bankrupt company applying for a job at another company will have to begin at a much reduced salary and can also expect significantly lower future retirement benefits. This is because Japanese companies generally do not reward work experience and seniority accumulated at other companies (see chapter 14).

Some workers stay late not necessarily to put in extra work, but for personal reasons. Staying late can mean avoiding rush-hour madness, working at a more comfortable pace, or being able to listen to the music you like while you're working. For some workers, staying late can even mean having beer while you work, or perhaps simply not making your wife angry by returning to a cramped house when the kids are still studying. Staying late at work also means not spending money to be somewhere else while you're waiting for an appropriate time to arrive home, and it means being where people can see you so they won't gossip about what you do between work hours and the time you arrive home. And, of course, staying late at work allows your wife to praise your diligence to the children, thereby instilling motivation in the children, who should take dad as an example of the kind of effort that they should be putting into their studying. Since companies may also want their workers to stay late, by actually staying late, workers satisfy both their personal and company goals.

How Do Management and Labor Cooperate to Promote Free Overtime?

Managers would be the first to suffer if their workers began to claim all their overtime. Article 36 of the national Labor Standard Law, entitled "overtime work and work on holidays," states that employers can require their employees to work overtime and on holidays only if both the union and management have an agreement on the maximum hours of allowable overtime. Individual companies and their unions have used that national agreement as a model to strike their own local agreements. The 1993 national labor–management agreement stipulates maximum overtime hours for male workers at fifteen hours per week, forty-five hours per month, and 360 hours per year. Managers cannot exceed those limits without violating the agreement. But in actual practice this agreement is almost universally disregarded. Unpaid overtime has become so widespread that it has become an institutionalized feature in the Japanese workplace.

What Happens When Service Overtime
Is Claimed as Real Overtime?

Anyone who attempts to "call a spade a spade" in order to get paid for what others call "service overtime" faces severe sanctions from his co-workers and management. In retaliation, he may be assigned "just to dig holes." That's the expression used when a worker is punished by being assigned no task, or a meaningless task, or he is ostracized by other workers. The resulting stress forces him to resign from the company. Such harassment is called *ibiri,* and is the workplace counterpart of the better-known *ijime,* or bullying, in Japanese schools.

Needless to say, one individual's deviant behavior is less threatening to a company than a collective demand from all employees to be paid for their overtime hours. Only a few lawsuits are ever brought against companies for exceeding the maximum overtime limits. In one such case in 1992, a Japanese bank was forced to provide back pay to its employees amounting to 195 million yen for the previous year's unpaid overtime because it had violated Article 37 of the Labor Standard Law, which stipulates that employers must pay a 25 percent premium for work performed on holidays and after normal hours.

What Will Happen When Workaholics Go on the Wagon?

The Japanese government wants to reduce the amount of free overtime in the workplace. A report prepared in 1994 for the Economic Planning Agency proposed to impose *jitan sokushin ryōkin,* or a "fee for promoting shorter hours." In effect, this proposal would assess a penalty on each firm unless it has a plan for shorter work hours for its employees and can prove the absence of unpaid overtime.

Workers are not optimistic that unpaid overtime will soon be eliminated. According to a recent survey conducted by the respected economics newspaper, *Nihon Keizai Shimbun,* most workers feel that there will be no change without an effective campaign to transform the workplace and people's attitudes. Indeed, as more Japanese companies switch from a system of lifetime employment to one of hiring by contract for fixed-term periods (see chapter 12), and as promotions and pay raises are increasingly based on merit rather than seniority (see chapter 14), Japanese employees may feel compelled to put in even more unpaid overtime to gain promotion or to keep their jobs.

14

How Do Workers
Get Paid?

Naoki Mitani

A midsummer visitor to Japan will be impressed by the throngs of people in boutiques and department stores shopping for presents. Japanese shoppers are observing their custom of buying midyear gifts for customers, supervisors, and others of higher rank to show their appreciation (see chapter 4).

Shoppers also spend a lot of money buying things—especially big-ticket items—for themselves. Travel agencies do a booming business selling package tours to domestic and foreign destinations at peak-season prices. This frenetic shopping just happens to coincide with the time of year when Japanese workers receive one of their large semiannual bonuses. They can expect to receive another large lump-sum bonus at the end of the year, and for many there is also a somewhat smaller bonus in March.

Many American workers also receive bonuses from their employers, typically at the end of the year. What's different in Japan is the large size of the bonus (relative to total compensation) and the regularity of payment. Japanese workers have come to regard their biannual lump-sum bonuses as part of their regular pay.

In addition to bonus payments, the Japanese compensation system has two other striking features: a wage profile that rises steeply with a worker's age, and lump-sum retirement payments. But to understand how Japanese workers are paid, you have to look beyond the individual components of Japanese pay to examine the entire compensation system.

Regular Earnings

A typical worker in firms with five or more employees received a monthly salary of 277,000 yen (about 2,770 U.S. dollars) in 1994. In addition, the worker received bonuses (summer and winter) amounting to a total of three-and-a-half months' salary, or about 971,000 yen (9,710 U.S. dollars). The monthly regular salary includes regular earnings (wages or salary) plus overtime. Regular earnings include the base wage and various allowances for commuting, dependents, and so on. These allowances were introduced just before World War II, when the government mobilized the economy for war and froze both wages and prices, and the corporations sought some flexibility by giving allowances to their employees. Employers were reluctant to increase the base wage, preferring the additional allowances; the unions were only concerned about total compensation, not by how it was divided. Today, wages are determined through collective bargaining each spring between employers and labor unions.

Shuntō (Spring Offensive)

Most Japanese labor unions are enterprise or company unions and include both blue- and white-collar workers. To increase their collective bargaining power, enterprise unions affiliate with industrial federation unions which, in turn, affiliate with national organizations. The largest of the national organizations is Rengo, the Japanese Trade Union Confederation, with 7.9 million members, representing 62 percent of all organized workers.

In 1955, workers in some industries began to coordinate their collective bargaining in the spring. This practice of coordinated labor contract negotiations during the spring of each year, or *shuntō* (Spring Offensive), has survived to this day. The *shuntō* system establishes an annual cycle corresponding to the Japanese fiscal year for both businesses and the government. The Spring Offensive is usually led by unions from the four heavy industries—iron and steel, ship-building, automobile, and electric machinery—which are affiliated with the Metal Workers Federation. Through these negotiations, the major corporations determine wages for the following year. These settlements also set the pattern for agreements in other industries. Agreements in the private sector are followed by wage adjustments in the public sector. The government also adjusts the minimum wage and public utility fees in line with the new agreements.

The *shuntō* system yields a number of economic benefits. First, the predictability of the cycle makes it easier for businesses to make forecasts and management decisions. Second, synchronization of wage settlements lessens the risk that a firm might lose market share due to a protracted labor dispute if negotiations were conducted company by company. Third, the *shuntō* system reduces total bargaining costs since wage settlements at the leading corporations set the pattern for smaller companies. Moreover, because these major companies also compete in international markets, the settlements are consistent with maintaining Japan's global economic competitiveness. Finally, *shuntō* allows management and labor to share information on where their companies and the macroeconomy are heading. It has also served as a forum for labor and business to lobby the government to change policies affecting labor–management relations.

Bonuses

Regular workers in Japan generally receive biannual bonuses, but bonuses vary more than the workers' base wages and salaries. The bonus system introduces flexibility into the Japanese compensation system because bonuses can be raised or lowered in accordance with company profitability and individual worker productivity. The size of the annual bonuses is often determined through collective bargaining. Over the years, workers have come to expect bonuses as part of their steady income. In fact, installment payment plans for major purchases are designed with small monthly payments but large bonus-related payments, and banks and charities do hefty campaigning during bonus seasons.

There are three different ways of looking at the bonus system. First, the bonus can be seen as a lump-sum payment of regular wages. This is how labor unions view it. According to this view, part of each employee's regular wages are withheld to be paid in a lump sum every six months. The stability of the ratio of bonuses to regular monthly contractual earnings would tend to support this view. This interpretation is further reinforced by the government's practice of paying about five months' salary as a bonus to public employees, regardless of individual worker performance or fiscal condition.

Second, the bonus can also be viewed as compensation contingent on the current performance of the company or individual. This view gains support from the fact that bonuses exhibit much greater variation over time and across companies and industries than regular wages. About six out of ten firms consider their profits to be the most important factor in determining the size of the bonus. Actually, the relationship between the two is relatively weak. A 10 percent increase in profits typically results in only about one percent increase in bonus payments and about 0.25 percent increase in total wages.

Third, the bonus system can also be seen as an incentive to individual workers to perform well on the job. Only 13 percent of bonuses paid reflect productivity of individual workers. Hence, the incentive role of the bonus system is limited.

Nenkō Age-Wage Curve

Wages increase with age and tenure. This relationship is called the *nenkō* age–wage curve. In Japan the slope of the *nenkō* curve is steeper for both white- and blue-collar workers than it is in other industrialized countries. A typical male worker aged forty-five to forty-nine gets 2.1 times more in monthly scheduled earnings than a similar male worker twenty-five years younger.

The steep Japanese age–wage profile is closely related to the long-term employment practices and the accumulation of skills within a company. Normally, entry-level workers are assigned to easier jobs and are transferred to related but more difficult jobs as they gain additional skills. When the acquired skills are firm-specific, the worker becomes more valuable to his company. As long as the worker continues to gain firm-specific skills, his wage rises in tandem with age and years of service with the company.

The steep age–wage profile also reflects the fact that a Japanese worker's wage is essentially comprised of two parts: one part is received today and the other part is received sometime in the future as deferred compensation. The problem for the worker is that if he leaves the company for whatever reason, he does not receive the deferred part of his compensation. Hence, the steep age–wage profile in Japan encourages the worker to continue to perform, improve his skills, *and* stay with his company.

The *nenkō* age–wage system is supported by two other features of the Japanese compensation system. First, unlike in the United States, wages in Japan are not related to specific jobs but to the qualifications of the workers. If wages were tied to specific jobs, job reassignments might result in a worker receiving lower wages. This would discourage job transfers and the opportunity to accumulate broader skills. Second, regular wage increases are also determined, to some extent, by merit, thus encouraging the worker to acquire additional skills.

Lump-Sum Retirement Payment

Large lump-sum payment at the time of compulsory retirement is the third feature of the Japanese compensation system. A male college graduate with thirty-five years of service or more is likely to get over 28 million yen (280,000 U.S. dollars) as a retirement allowance. This amounts to four years of pay. A high school graduate with the same number of years of service can expect about 17 million yen at retirement. These lump-sum payments are the primary source of retirement income for most people. The size of the lump-sum payment increases disproportionately with years of service, again encouraging workers to stay with their companies. Large companies also tend to be more generous than small companies. Because of Japan's aging workforce, more than half of the companies plan to replace this lump-sum payment system with a pension system and allow their employees to choose between the two. Japan's tax code favors the pension system over lump-sum payments.

Future Directions

Some people are not happy with Japan's labor compensation system. The *nenkō* curve does not apply to most workers in small companies. It is also of no benefit to most employed women, who find few opportunities to improve their work skills within Japanese companies. Typically, women leave the company after only a few years and lose the chance of ever earning the higher wages that are associated with long-term employment. Gender and age discrimination in the workplace continue to plague women and the elderly regardless of their qualifications. With a rapid increase in the number of aged in its population, Japan may have to reform the current compensation system.

Some also question whether the benefits of the *shuntō* system outweigh its costs. While huge amounts of resources are spent in reaching new agreements each spring, recent agreements show little difference from automatic annual wage adjustments based on seniority. The wisdom of all companies following the pattern of wage settlements set by large corporations is also questionable when there are large differences in labor productivity among industries and companies.

Japanese companies are beginning to change the ways they pay their employees. In the 1997 spring labor agreement, Toyota Motor Corporation broke ranks with its rivals by offering higher wages to its employees.

Faced with slower economic growth, Japanese companies are also experimenting with labor compensation based on individual performance in order to improve efficiency, thus deemphasizing age and seniority. The 1997 spring labor-management agreement gave smaller across-the-board annual wage increases, allowing companies to implement a performance-based system that rewards workers with a yearly bonus. Companies have been using "merit" to determine part of an employee's wages, but often they have not adequately distinguished between ability and performance. Japan's labor unions may have to play a greater role in guiding the ways in which individual performance based pay systems, especially for white-collar workers, are designed and implemented by management.

15

Do the Japanese Work till They Drop?

Yoshitaka Fukui

The stereotype of the Japanese male worker is the workaholic who spends long hours at work, frequently works on weekends, and hardly ever takes a long vacation or spends much time with his family. Some are believed to die suddenly from overwork *(karōshi)*. Indeed, each year about five hundred families file workmen's compensation claims for *karōshi*, although only about 5 to 7 percent of these claims are ultimately approved by the government. Some families have also filed lawsuits against employers alleging their relatives were worked to death. Anecdotes of long work hours abound, but I don't believe that they accurately portray the current work habits of most Japanese employees.

The Data

Before World War II, Japanese manufacturing production workers put in grueling, long hours. In the 1930s, it was not unusual for factory workers in Japan to work twelve hours a day except on Sunday. But times have changed. In 1985, Japanese manufacturing production workers still put in more hours (2,168) per year than workers in the United States (1,929 annual hours) and in major European countries. However, in 1994 and in a weak

Taking a day off

More companies are implementing five-day work weeks instead of the six-or-more-days' work week. Here is a breakdown of the increase.

FIRMS WITH 5-DAY WORK WEEKS	1984	1994
Every week	6.7%	20.3%
Once or more per month	51.2%	87.0%
WORKERS WITH 5-DAY WORK WEEKS		
Every week	27.0%	52.9%
Once or more per month	51.2%	95.2%

Source: Ministry
of Labor

December

SUNDAY	MONDAY	TUESDAY	WEDNESDAY	THURSDAY	FRIDAY	SATURDAY
	1 Work	2 Work	3 Work	4 Work	5 Work	6 Work Day off
7 Day off	8 Work	9 Work	10 Work	11 Work	12 Work	13 Work Day off
	15	16 Work	17 Work	18 Work	19 Work	20 Work Day off
					26	27

economy, Japanese production workers actually worked fewer hours (1,966 hours) than American workers (2,005 hours).

Manufacturing workers are not the only workers laboring fewer hours in Japan. In 1995, manufacturing workers averaged 164 hours per month compared to 159 hours for all workers. Only workers in mining, transportation and communication, and construction worked more hours.

The decline in Japanese work hours coincides with the change in the country's labor law, which reduced the maximum normal working hours from 48 in 1947 to 40 hours per week today. The 5-day work week, instead of the 5.5- or 6-day work week, has become the norm for most workers. Japanese workers are also getting more holidays each year. In 1994, the typical Japanese manufacturing worker had 124 days off from work (including weekends) compared to 132 days for the U.S. worker. All together, data do not support the claim of exceptionally long work hours in Japan today. Of course, there are problems in comparing official data reported by different countries, which may measure work hours differently.

Unpaid Overtime

In Japan, working overtime is a common workplace practice. In 1995, Japanese workers averaged 159 hours of work per month; eleven of those hours were paid overtime. Generally, all male university graduates newly hired by Japanese companies are placed on a career path with expectations of being groomed for management positions. But promotion in large Japanese corporations is an incrementally slow process (though it is fast in small firms). It may take a man ten years or more to reach the level of section head *(kachō)*; until then, even a white-collar salaried management trainee qualifies for overtime pay. Companies normally budget for overtime, but many Japanese salarymen exceed their overtime allowances and put in extra hours often by working late into the evening without pay. This phenomenon is called "service overtime" or unpaid overtime (see chapter 13). Financial institutions are notorious for alleged long work hours and service overtime (and *short* customer hours!). Service overtime is rare among OLs (office ladies), who are considered non-career track workers, and among factory workers. To the extent unpaid overtime is not officially recorded, statistics may understate the actual number of hours worked.

When Do They Go Home?

A not uncommon story in the April 30, 1997 issue of the *International Herald Tribune* describes the typical scene at a Japanese company or government bureaucracy after normal working hours:

> Call a Japanese office at 10 P.M. and chances are excellent that someone will pick up the phone. As Japan tries to cast off its post-war business culture, one of the hardest habits to break is the famous addiction to marathon hours. Around the country, when darkness falls, white-collar workers keep right on going. Some work, some doze, some sit around their desks and eat and talk baseball. What they do not do is go home. . . .
>
> The scene at the Ministry of Finance one recent evening after 10 is played out in many Japanese offices. Lights were blazing all over the building. In some rooms men sat hunched over their desks, sleeves rolled up, churning through documents. In others, groups of colleagues chatted, laughed and drank sodas. Outside each office were stacks of dirty plates, with bits of take-out Chinese food and sushi scattered about. Rushing into the hallway to buy a drink from a vending machine, a 25-year old bureaucrat declared, "I'm just gearing up." Nearby, a weary 23-year old from the securities bureau shrugged as he got into an elevator, saying, "I'll be here until 4 A.M."

A government report recently described Japanese salarymen as "corporate servants" rather than corporate employees. Is it true that all, or perhaps even most, Japanese salarymen work long hours and stay late after normal working hours as is widely portrayed by the news media, in movies, and in television soap operas? The question could be answered by taking a survey of companies to see who arrives and leaves at what time each work day. Unfortunately, such data are not available.

Another option is to check the subway train schedules. Every worker must commute between home and office unless he lives in his office. Since almost all workers in the central Tokyo business district commute by train or subway, we can infer their work schedules by looking at the train or subway schedules. Punctuality of Japanese trains and subways is legendary.

For example, Otemachi Station of the subway Marunouchi Line is located in the heart of corporate Japan, and this line is one of the busiest in Japan. For comparison, pick Line 7 at Grand Central Station in New York City. The number of trains leaving these stations during each hour (as a fraction of all trains leaving during a twenty-four-hour day) during weekdays has been plotted in figure 1a. In figure 1a, 8 A.M. means the trains leave between 8.00 A.M. and 9.00 A.M. Typical office hours in Tokyo (and Japan) are from 9 A.M. to around 6 P.M., and train frequency at Marunouchi Station matches this pattern surprisingly well. The train frequency profile of Marunouchi is also very similar to that at Grand Central Station in New York. Figures 1b and 1c compare the Saturday and Sunday train frequency profiles at Marunouchi and Grand Central, and show them to be very similar, though compared to weekdays, the weekend traffic peak is much lower. Similar results are found when we compare Tozai and Chiyoda lines in Tokyo and Lines 6 and S at New York's Grand Central.

This simple comparison of train schedules suggests that most office workers in the Tokyo central business district arrive at their offices before 9 A.M. and leave a little after the workday ends around 6 P.M. (A one-hour lunch break is not counted in hours of work. Japanese labor law requires at least forty-five minutes of unpaid free time during the lunch period if employees work more than six hours in the day.) The evening traffic peaks between 6 and 7 P.M., and the height of the evening peak suggests that it is not just the office ladies—who make up about half of the central business district workforce—who are leaving at that hour. The Tokyo subway train schedules suggest that the majority of the Japanese office workers are not leaving their offices at 10 P.M. or just before the last train at midnight.

Some Japanese male office workers no doubt work late and long hours, but so do many American workers. According to

Figure 1: Percent of Daily Subway Service by the Hour in Tokyo and New York

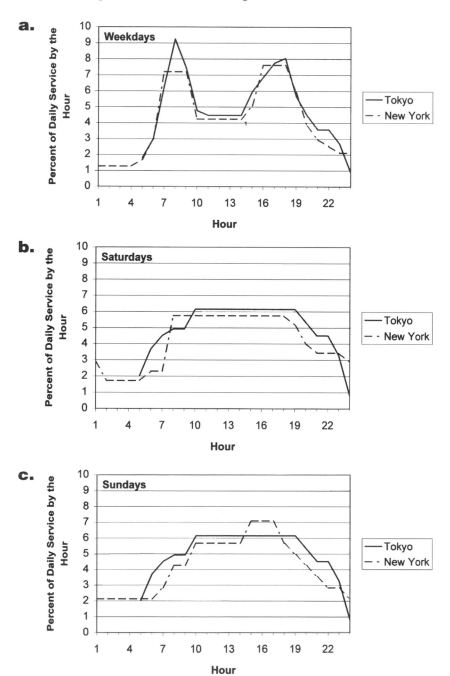

the U.S. Bureau of Labor Statistics, 20 percent of the American nonagricultural workforce (including part-time workers) work more than forty-nine hours each week, and 8 percent work more than sixty hours per week.

Train frequency data have limitations. The number of riders per train is higher during rush hours. However, the queuing restriction to avoid hypercongestion on the Chuo Line platform at JR Tokyo Station (the closest JR train station to Otemachi area) ends between 6:30 P.M. and 7 P.M., suggesting that after 7 P.M. the commuter traffic diminishes.

It is widely believed that male workers, even if they don't stay at their desks after normal working hours, may be entertaining customers or discussing business with colleagues over food and drink in nearby restaurants. (That might also be an excuse given to wives by late-returning husbands!) Having missed the last train at midnight, they go home by taxi. However, Tokyo's fifty thousand taxis can only carry an insignificant fraction of the city's 6 million workers even if only male salarymen stayed out late. A recent Japanese television program showed a large number of people waiting in the early morning hours for the gate at Roppongi Station of the subway Hibiya Line to open so they could catch the first train home. However, these people were not going home from work; they were going home after a night of revelry in one of Tokyo's most popular entertainment districts.

Does Reality Match Perception?

Why do so many people believe that long work hours is the Japanese norm? Perhaps it is a relic from the postwar decades, when there was more than a grain of truth to this belief. Japanese manufacturing workers were still working 2,400 hours per year in the early 1960s and 2,200 hours in the 1980s. The train schedule on Saturdays used to be the same as on weekdays. Banks and government offices have been on a five-day work week since 1992, though public schools are still in session two Saturdays a month. Since April 1997, the forty-hour standard work week has been extended to virtually all employees. Thus, a careful examination of the data finds that Japanese are working fewer hours today, but the stereotype of the workaholic Japanese salaryman hasn't changed. Japanese workers are definitely working fewer days in the year. Perhaps some salarymen are still working long hours daily, or at least staying late at the office; and maybe everyone works long hours occasionally. But the train schedules suggest that not all, or even most, Japanese salarymen are routinely putting in marathon hours!

16

Why Do the Japanese Save So Much?

Charles Yuji Horioka

According to official government statistics, Japanese households saved one-sixth of their after-tax incomes on average between 1960 and 1994. In some years the savings rate was almost one-fourth of their incomes. By contrast, American households saved a modest 7.1 percent of their incomes on average during the same period. Thus, the savings rate among Japanese households appears to be more than twice that of American households and nearly 10 percentage points higher. The government statistics suggest that the Japanese are much bigger savers than Americans. Is this really true?

Are the Japanese Really Big Savers?

Comparing official statistics on household savings from different countries can yield misleading conclusions because the measures of savings used in the different countries are not always comparable. My own calculations show that, after making the proper adjustments, the Japanese still save a higher percentage of their incomes than Americans, but the difference in their saving rates is only half as large as official statistics suggest.

The Japanese also save a higher percentage of their after-tax incomes than the *average* among households in all countries. However, there are many countries—including China, Indone-

sia, South Korea, Malaysia, Singapore, Taiwan, and Thailand in Asia, along with Greece, Italy, and Switzerland in Europe—whose residents save as much, if not more, of their after-tax incomes as the Japanese.

Moreover, Japan's household savings rate has taken a plunge since peaking at about 23 percent between 1974 and 1976. It was only 12.8 percent in 1994, the most recent year for which data are available. In other words, Japan's household savings rate has fallen by almost one-half in less than two decades.

To sum up, Japan's household savings rate is not as high as the official government figures suggest nor is it as high as it used to be; it is certainly not the highest in the world, but it is higher than in the United States and also higher than the average among all countries. So the answer to the question about whether the Japanese are really such big savers is a qualified "yes."

Why Do the Japanese Save So Much?

One popular theory attributes Japan's high household savings rate to culture, tradition, or national character. It argues that

Japanese are prolific savers because frugality is a virtue according to Confucian teachings. Culturalist explanations are hard to confirm or refute, but the fact that Japan's household savings rate was not always high (it was low and often *negative* before World War II) suggests that culture is *not* the dominant explanation.

What, then, are the reasons for Japan's high household savings rate? Nearly forty factors have been suggested as possible candidates, but I list only the eight most frequently cited factors.

(1) *The high rate of economic growth.* The Japanese economy grew at double-digit rates during the 1950s, 1960s, and early 1970s. During that period of rapid economic growth, household incomes were rising so rapidly that the Japanese could not adjust their spending habits fast enough to keep pace with their rising incomes. The result was an increase in savings, since income that is not spent is, by definition, saved.

(2) *The low level of assets.* Much of Japan's housing inventory was destroyed during World War II, while the real value of household financial assets such as cash and savings accounts was greatly reduced by the postwar hyperinflation. For both reasons, household assets in Japan were at a very low level just after the war. Thus, one factor motivating Japanese households to save so much might have been the desire to restore their assets to previous levels.

(3) *The low level of social security benefits.* The level of social security benefits in Japan was relatively low until the early 1970s, and this may have induced Japanese households to save more in preparation for future retirement.

(4) *The unavailability of consumer credit.* Until recently, consumer credit was difficult to obtain in Japan, and this also may have induced Japanese households to save up in advance before buying big-ticket items such as housing, automobiles, furniture, and household appliances.

(5) *Tax breaks for saving.* The Japanese tax system also encouraged people to save. For example, under the *maruyū* system interest income was tax-exempt up to a certain limit.

(6) *The bonus system.* A considerable portion of Japanese employee compensation is paid in the form of large biannual lump-sum bonuses (see chapter 14). Some scholars believe that this method of compensation encourages or, at least, makes it easier for people to save.

(7) *Government promotion of saving.* The Japanese government, as well as the Central Council for Savings Promotion, a quasi-government agency affiliated with the Bank of Japan, engaged in various activities that encouraged people to save. These activities included setting up model savings districts and groups, children's banks, training courses for working youths, producing savings-promoting publications and films, and so on.

(8) *Youthful population.* People typically work and save when they are young; when they become old, they retire and live off their previously accumulated savings. Thus, the country's overall household savings rate will be higher the more young people there are relative to the number of old people. Until recently, the age structure of Japan's population was the youngest among the developed countries, and this could well have been a major explanation for Japan's high household savings rate.

Will the Japanese Always Be Big Savers?

Most of the factors that explain Japan's high savings rate no longer apply. Economic growth rates have been much lower in recent years, household ownership of assets is much higher than it used to be, social security benefits were greatly improved in the early 1970s, consumer credit has become much more readily available, most tax breaks on savings were abolished in 1988, the government has discontinued its savings-promotion activities, with the Central Council for Savings Promotion being renamed the Central Council for Savings Information in 1988, and, most important, Japan's population is aging rapidly. Thus, it is hardly surprising that Japan's household savings rate has plunged since the mid-1970s.

Moreover, this downward trend is likely to continue and even accelerate as the reasons for Japan's high household savings rate become even less applicable. For one thing, the proportion of the elderly in the total population is growing at a faster pace than in any other country. By the year 2010, Japan will be the most aged society in the world. My simulations and those of others suggest that, by then, Japan's household saving rate will be zero or even negative. In other words, Japanese households may, on average, be spending more than their incomes in the not-too-distant future.

Does It Matter How Much the Japanese Save?

How much a person saves is, of course, important to the person doing the saving because it determines whether or not there are sufficient funds available for unexpected contingencies, retirement, and so on. But savings are also important for the economy because they provide the funds needed to finance investment in factories, office buildings and equipment, highways, schools, housing, and the like. The Japanese economy grew rapidly during the high-growth period, largely because ample savings were available to finance investment which, in turn, expanded the productive capacity of the economy.

Does this mean that the sharp decline in Japan's household savings rate will have dire consequences for the Japanese economy and its population's future standard of living? Not necessarily (see chapter 1). Japan's population is not only aging; its growth rate is tapering off as well. By around 2010, the Japanese population is expected to begin declining, and a declining population means that there will be less need to expand the productive capacity of the economy and therefore less need for investment. And because the decline in the household savings rate will be accompanied by a decline in domestic investment demand, a savings shortage will not necessarily develop in Japan.

However, there is growing concern that the continued decline in the Japanese savings rate may bring about a *worldwide* savings shortage. The Japanese have saved more than they were able to invest in their own country, and the leftover savings have flowed abroad, helping alleviate savings shortages in the United States and other countries. The decline in Japan's household savings rate will reduce the amount of savings that Japan can supply to the rest of the world, and this, in turn, may precipitate a worldwide savings shortage. But other countries (such as the East Asian and Southeast Asian countries) have recently shown dramatic increases in their savings rates and they may be able to make up for the decline in Japanese saving. Nonetheless, since the world's investment needs are expected to remain high for the foreseeable future, especially in the formerly socialist economies and the developing countries, it would be better for the rest of the world if the decline in Japan's household savings rate was as gradual as possible.

System

17

Why Is Japan
a Paradise of
Vending Machines?

Robert Parry

Hike to some of Japan's oldest Buddhist temples secluded among dense alpine forests, stroll along the shores of Okinawa's coral islands, or indeed go anywhere in Japan and it soon becomes clear that, regardless of all the clichés and stereotypes about the country, Japan should actually be known as the paradise of vending machines on Earth. Indeed, there are so many machines that they soon blend into the landscape and get taken for granted as a part of everyday life.

Apart from the enormous number of machines selling soft drinks and cigarettes, it is also possible to buy alcohol, candy and ice cream, instant soup noodles *(ramen)*, pornographic magazines and videotapes, towels and underwear (in case you forget to take some with you to a public bath), flowers, batteries, photographic film, and fresh (?) eggs. Some shrines even have machines that, for 200 yen (about 2 U.S. dollars), will issue a slip of paper purporting to tell your fortune, surely the next best thing to owning presses to print money.

There are currently around 5.4 million vending machines in Japan, about one for every twenty-two people. Placed next to each other, they would practically form two rows from the

southern tip of Kyushu to the northern tip of Hokkaido. The total annual sales from the machines are in excess of 6.4 trillion yen (about 64 billion U.S. dollars). Only half the machines sell drinks. Japan has twice as many vending machines dispensing drinks and four times as much sales volume per person as the United States, the runner-up in the vending machine race.

Why Are Vending Machines So Popular?

A good part of the popularity of vending machines is a consequence of high land prices, high labor costs, and low crime rates. Japan's mountainous geography and protectionist agricultural policy keep urban land prices high (see chapter 8). Vending machines produce more revenue from each square meter of scarce land than a retail store can. With spectacular postwar economic growth, labor costs in Japan sky-rocketed. Even the cheapest labor for hire (students working part-time) costs about 800 yen (8 U.S. dollars) per hour. Vending machines need only a periodic visit from the operator to replenish the supplies and empty the cash.

Close observation of the vending machine business, however, suggests that a major factor accounting for such a huge number of machines is simply the remarkable lack of crime in Japan. The incidence of vandalism and theft is so low in Japan that even though most machines are located outdoors, often on sidewalks, it is rare to see a vandalized machine. Though a large machine may contain up to 80,000 yen (800 U.S. dollars) in cash, even in isolated areas where alarm systems are hardly effective and the machines themselves can be carted away for resale, vending machines are not targets. Japan does not assemble data on machine-related crime, but one operator of two thousand machines reported only five (or 0.25 percent) incidents of vandalism in 1994. For fear of vandalism, American vending machine companies don't even consider operating stand-alone, street-side units.

Adaptation of vending machines to dispense a broad range of merchandise is another factor that helps explain their popularity. Canned coffee, a product unique to Japan, provides a good example. Sales of cold drinks, the mainstay of vending machines in Japan's sweltering summer heat, not surprisingly sag in winter. However, in 1969, the UCC company produced coffee in a can that could be sold either hot or cold. This technological breakthrough freed the coffee machines from the need for water supply. The idea quickly caught on with the public, as well as with UCC's competitors. The innovation helped triple the number of machines in five years, with a sixfold increase in fifteen years. But today, Coca-Cola's Georgia has become the dominant brand in the Japanese canned coffee market.

Uniform Prices

In the United States, a vending machine located at a gas station might sell its soft drinks for a different price than one located at a supermarket. By contrast, many visitors to Japan are surprised that vending machines almost everywhere sell canned drinks at the same price (110 yen, but still 100 yen in most places in Okinawa, though 250 yen is not unusual at isolated resort hotels and at congested tee-grounds on the golf links). Obviously, vending machine operators don't compete on the basis of price. Why not? And on what basis do they compete?

People rarely go to a vending machine to buy products that they take home and consume later. This makes the location of a machine and the products it contains the most important factors in determining the volume of sales. A machine at the entrance to a cafeteria generates much higher sales than a machine selling similar merchandise just a few meters away. Given the importance of location, vending machine operators, especially the drink manufacturers and distributors, compete vigorously by offering attractive financial terms to the owners of high-volume sites. Surprisingly, despite differences in rents paid to site owners, vending machine operators charge the same price for canned drinks in all their machines.

In Japan, vendors prefer to compete on location and product variety rather than on price. Since consumers are believed not to want to go the extra distance to pay a lower price, why charge a different price? In Japan, higher-priced products also carry the image of high quality, making it less attractive for vendors to compete on price. Since many of the machines are operated by manufacturers of the products sold in them, the manufacturers want to control and maintain the retail price directly. It is not unusual for a manufacturer to take the illegal stance of threatening to cut off the distributor/operator unless he or she agrees to maintain the suggested retail price.

In order to compete on price, a vendor of canned drinks must find an alternative source of cheaper drinks. A strong yen has made that possible. Discount retailers are now offering cheaper, mostly U.S.-made, drinks sold under the retailers' own house brands in vending machines outside their stores. Richard Branson's Virgin Group is selling a cola produced in New Zealand at the standard 110-yen price, but in a larger can. Some very small distributors are selling brand-name imports at a discount. However, market penetration of these discounters is slow, they lack a large distribution network, and good sites are already saturated with machines.

Proliferation of New Products

Competition in the introduction of new products is ferocious. For example, the major producers each offer, at any one time, around thirty different (nonalcoholic) beverages, including about ten types of coffee using different combinations of beans and production methods. In one two-year period in the 1980s, more than 140 new types of coffee were introduced.

Many other types of beverage have also proliferated. These include fruit juices, quasi-medicinal health drinks, and isotonic sports drinks, one of the most popular brands in the latter category having been named Pocari Sweat. Since 1991, the Health and Welfare Ministry has permitted various health drinks (such as Fibe-Mini, which claims to furnish one day's requirement of dietary fiber) and numerous energy-providing pep drinks to be advertised as health products.

Indeed, a good part of the vendors' incomes seems to be spent in developing, introducing, and promoting an incredible variety of products. Commercials for canned drinks continually blitz television and radio, sometimes attracting a cult following. Famous entertainers—including foreign movie stars—are recruited to sell products. Japan's leading brewer, Kirin, has hired Los Angeles Dodgers strikeout sensation, Hideo Nomo, to pitch its *Jive* coffee.

Vending machine operators also segment the market by preferences and location. Young women, it seems, have a sweet tooth and blue-collar men prefer bitter tastes; the contents of vending machines in a women's college and at a truck stop are differentiated accordingly.

The Negative Side of Vending Machines

Vending machines generate litter in a country with a scarcity of refuse bins. For vehicular passengers waiting at a traffic light, drainage pipes in embankment walls an arm's length away apparently seemed to offer a convenient receptacle, one which would later be less conveniently emptied, especially when the cans emerge at missile speeds during typhoons. Most new vending machines now include a receptacle, as Japan joins the recycling movement.

Japan was apparently slow to wake up to this problem of litter. Throw-away tabs on pop-top cans were the norm for canned beverages until the early 1990s, American products with pushdown tops having led the way. Japan may be ahead in the proliferation of vending machines, but is a full generation behind in adjusting to some of the potential problems.

There have also been some recent moves to regulate the proliferation of vending machines. Their placement in public spaces, such as sidewalks, may be restricted. Also, the access of minors to alcohol and cigarettes dispensed from unattended machines has become a matter of concern. In theory at least, machines that sell alcohol are supposed to shut down from 11 P.M. to 5 A.M. The industry has bowed to public pressure and has agreed to remove by the year 2000 all alcohol-dispensing machines located outside liquor stores, or to introduce an identity-card system. Similar moves are afoot to place restrictions on the sale of cigarettes.

Will vending machines ever be as popular in the rest of the world as in Japan? Perhaps not, unless the rest of the world can achieve comparably low crime rates. An argument has been made that the Japanese acceptance of canned coffee and tea may not transplant well to the West, which has its own well-established coffee and tea culture. But don't be so sure. If karaoke has been successfully transplanted to the West. . . .

18

Why Do Doctors Prescribe So Many Pills?

Akihiko Kawaura and
Sumner J. LaCroix

A visit to the doctor in Japan is rarely complete until the doctor has prescribed large amounts of medicine to treat the patient's condition. Chances are good that the patient will leave the doctor's office with several prescriptions. It is relatively common to see a patient receiving as many as four to five kinds of pills, packets, and capsules to take three times a day. Why do Japanese doctors prescribe so many drugs? It is certainly not because Japanese patients have a peculiarly high demand for medicine. The answer is likely to be found by focusing on the behavior of doctors. We believe that the intensive use of drugs in Japan is primarily due to the incentives offered to Japanese doctors practicing under the country's health insurance system.

Share of Drug Expenditures in
National Health Care Spending

One distinctive feature of Japanese medical spending is that expenditures on medicine have constituted a very high percentage of total health care spending. It is estimated that in the early

1970s more than 40 percent of the total health care bill was accounted for by prescription and injectable drugs. Although the expenditure share of drugs had fallen to 27 percent by 1994, Japan's per capita use of the latest generation of antibiotic drugs is greater than anywhere else in the world. In the United States, the spending on drugs amounted to about 11 percent of health care expenditures in 1993. If we adjust for differences in health care expenditures per person across the two countries, we still find that the Japanese spend a larger proportion of gross domestic product (GDP) on medicine than Americans.

Screening a New Patient

One of the reasons for the emphasis on prescriptions in Japan is that Japanese doctors are inundated with patients. In 1961, Japan established a health insurance system that covered its entire population (see chapter 21). There are currently three main sources of health insurance: (1) public and private insurance plans for employees and their dependents, (2) public insurance plans for self-employed persons and their dependents, and (3) a public insurance plan for senior citizens. In 1992, patients shouldered about 12 percent of health care spending, with the remainder picked up by the three insurance plans. These insurance systems have reduced the out-of-pocket cost to a patient visiting a doctor. The result is that doctors are flooded with patients. The average physician in a clinic in Japan sees three to four times more patients per day than a U.S. physician. In order to manage this flood of patients, doctors in Japan use simple medications to screen patients with more serious conditions.

For example, when a doctor treats a patient with flu symptoms, he usually begins by dispensing ordinary medicines that control the fever, runny nose, and cough. At this stage, he does not spend too much time hearing about the new patient's problem, since doing so will make it impossible to see all the other patients waiting for him. Physicians typically spend an average of three to five minutes with each patient. By comparison, a typical doctor in the United States spends twenty minutes with each patient. Many doctors do not give appointments to patients in Japan, so patients have to wait their turn. At major Japanese hospitals, patients sometimes wait one to three hours to see a doctor.

Essentially, most patients presenting relatively routine symptoms are sent away quickly with several prescriptions. This enables the doctors to ration their large patient loads and is one of the reasons behind the extensive use of prescriptions in Japan. Not surprisingly, patients with serious health problems will return after a few days because the first set of pills was ineffective in alleviating their problems. Doctors spend more time with each patient at the second visit to determine whether the illness is serious.

Government Policy toward Professional Medical Service

Another factor behind the high spending on drugs in Japan is the bias in public policy against other types of medical care. Insurance funds reimburse doctors according to points (one point is worth 10 yen) specified by the Ministry of Health and Welfare (MOHW). The points have been biased in favor of drug prescription and have discouraged doctors from spending a lot of time with each patient.

During the 1960s and 1970s, national health care expenditures increased annually at double-digit rates. The sharp increases alarmed the government, which feared that the insurance plans would go broke. The MOHW has since tried to contain health care spending, and services provided by doctors have been an easy target.

According to one estimate, the regulated price of medical service is only 33 percent to 50 percent of the price that doctors can charge for medical services to individuals who pay their own bills (to avoid restrictions placed on doctors by the insurance funds). The imposition of price controls on medical services provided doctors, especially those who work in private clinics and hospitals, with incentives to shy away from regulated time-intensive medical services and turn to other less time-intensive services, such as drug prescriptions.

The Drug–Price Gap

Another incentive for doctors to prescribe more medicine is the so-called drug–price gap. When doctors prescribe drugs, their patients often buy them from in-hospital (or in-clinic) pharmacies. Doctors receive reimbursements from insurance funds according to points specified by the prescribed drug. However, doctors regularly procure drugs at substantial discounts from the reimbursement price through negotiations with salespersons from the drug companies. A recent estimate puts this "gap" at about 1 trillion yen (about 10 billion U.S. dollars) out of the total expenditures on drugs of 7 trillion yen per year. While some of this "drug–price gap" covers the cost of operating in-clinic pharmacies, the remainder becomes part of the profits earned by hospitals, clinics, and doctors.

The MOHW has been aware of this price gap and has regularly adjusted the points for prescription drugs downward. During the 1960s and 1970s, the downward adjustment was, however, matched by a decline in the market price of many drugs, thereby maintaining the drug–price gap as well as doctors' incentives to rely on drug prescription.

Future Trends

Will doctors begin to prescribe fewer pills in Japan? It seems likely. Incentives provided by public policy have been greatly altered in recent years. Throughout the 1980s and 1990s, MOHW has increased the points awarded for professional services and decreased the points awarded for prescription drugs.

The government has been committed to closing the "drug–price gap" since the early 1980s. The drug price used as the basis for reimbursement was reduced by 18.6 percent in 1981, 16.6 percent in 1984, 10.2 percent in 1988, 9.2 percent in 1990, 6.6 percent in 1994, and 6.8 percent in 1996. A MOHW advisory group produced a report in 1996 that calls for an overhaul of the reimbursement system to eliminate the price gap completely by the year 2000. Two major obvious consequences have been witnessed so far: (1) a relative shift by drug manufacturers to over-the-counter (OTC) drug markets, and (2) the growth of independent pharmacies, which specialize in dispensing pills according to doctors' prescriptions.

First, since doctors have incentives to maintain the drug–price gap, they have demanded further discounts from drug manufacturers to compensate for the reduced reimbursement from government insurance plans. This has led some drug companies to put more resources into OTC drugs, which are, in some instances, reasonable substitutes for prescription drugs. Second, the vanishing drug–price gap has made in-house dispensing of drugs increasingly less attractive for doctors, who used to insist that patients purchase their pills from in-house pharmacies. Separation of prescription and dispensing has always been allowed, but it is likely that a move in this direction will gain momentum in the near future. The percentage of drugs dispensed outside hospitals was about 20 percent in 1995, and the MOHW predicts that this ratio will reach 50 percent during the 2010s.

The change in the points assigned to prescription drugs and patient services is consistent with Japan's ascendance to the highest level of economic development and per capita income. With patients assigning increased value to extending life and to obtaining a higher quality of life, they are beginning to demand that doctors spend more time attending to their health needs instead of just supplying them with pills. Such changes will, however, only result in longer lines at the doctor's office unless either the supply of doctors and other health care facilities is increased, enabling patients to receive better care, or demand is reduced by asking patients to pay a larger share of the cost of their doctor visits.

19

Why Do Bank Automatic Teller Machines Shut Down at 7 P.M.?

Shyam Sunder

The day after I arrived in Kobe, Japan, in May 1995, I opened a bank account. My English-speaking secretary patiently explained to me the routine rules of banking. She informed me that the weekday service hours of the bank's automatic teller machines (ATMs) are as follows:

From 9 A.M. to 6 P.M.:	No charge for ATM transactions
From 6 P.M. to 7 P.M.:	103 yen per transaction
From 7 P.M. to 9 A.M.:	Closed
Saturday:	Limited hours

Japan has been a leader in both the development and adoption of ATM technology. From 1969 to 1995, private banks in Japan installed about 105,000 machines. In addition, the Postal Savings Office (see chapter 22) has about 23,000 machines. In 1975, private banks started a joint venture company called Nippon Cash Service to allow some banks to share machines. Japan's ATM machines represent an investment of over one trillion yen (10 billion U.S. dollars). ATMs cut the cost of handling routine cash withdrawal and deposit transactions by a factor of about 10. Consequently, banks in Japan, as elsewhere, prefer that customers conduct their transactions on machines. Many Japanese machines offer advanced technical features (e.g., hot pressed and cleaned notes) and bank customers, especially the young, like to use ATMs. Having incurred the substantial fixed costs of putting machines in, why would the banks limit their service hours? In contrast, machines that allow you to borrow money against your credit card, or even take out a car loan, are open twenty-four hours a day. Over my three months' stay in Japan during the summer of 1995, I asked the same question of many of my friends and acquaintances. They suggested several possibilities.

Why Such Limited ATM Hours?

- It would be inconvenient for the bank staff to keep ATMs open at night.
- It would be unsafe to have ATMs open at night.
- Bank employees oppose longer hours for ATMs because it will reduce employment.
- Japanese people do not need to withdraw cash from ATMs in the evenings or weekends.
- Banks have insufficient computing capacity; they need the computers at night to update the ledgers, so they shut down the ATMs.
- It is no problem for my wife to go to the bank during the day to withdraw the cash we need.
- If the ATM runs out of cash in the evening or weekends or breaks down, there will be no one to service the machine.
- Japan's government (Ministry of Finance) does not allow the banks to extend ATM hours.
- The six major banks in Japan, instead of competing by offering better services to consumers, act like a big cartel.

There is at least some truth to most of these explanations.

Convenience of Staff

It would indeed be inconvenient for the bank staff to keep the ATMs open after hours. The ATM lobbies in Japanese banks often have attendants who greet customers on arrival and offer any help that may be needed. The need for help has generally disappeared as customers quickly learned to use the machines for routine functions soon after they were introduced, but the staff and the greetings remain. If around-the-clock ATM service also meant around-the-clock staff attendance, it would indeed be inconvenient for the staff.

Why staff the ATM machines? Having staff at the machines eliminates a good part of the economic advantage of ATMs, and also limits their hours. The explanation offered is that the Japanese demand and expect a high level of service from their retail establishments. It is easy to confirm this level of service and quality in department stores, hotels, restaurants, and shops, and virtually everywhere else. For example, department stores assign women employees to push elevator buttons in automated elevators and to announce the floor level and the major departments on each floor even though there are lighted signs in the elevators and just about everyone in Japan is literate.

Demand for High Level of Service

Whether Japanese consumers actually demand this high level of service with the attendant high prices is not clear. We would not know until retail establishments that deliver low-quality and less service at lower prices enter the market. Crowds at Daiei discount supermarkets seem to suggest that not all Japanese belong to the Bloomingdale set. Given a choice, many will pick cheaper goods and services. Not all Japanese consumers may want to have ATM attendants standing around. Some may prefer longer ATM hours instead. Why isn't this choice available?

Security

Concern about safety of nighttime operation of ATMs was surprising. Japan is, without question, among the safest places in the world to live, even after counting the Tokyo subway gassing by the Aum Shinrikyo sect just before I arrived in Japan. The Japanese are very much aware of this difference in living environment, especially in comparison to the United States, which is widely seen as an unsafe place to live. My friends did not know of a bank robbery, or of a bank customer being robbed after withdrawing money from the bank, even though the Japanese routinely withdraw and carry large amounts of cash. In Japan, where cash is still preferred over credit cards for routine purchases, it is not unusual to carry a thousand U.S. dollars' worth of currency in one's wallet. Yet, the concern about the safety of nighttime ATM operation was the most frequently given reason for their shutdown at 7 P.M.

In addition to the safety of the customers, banks could be concerned about the safety of the machines. At Sakura Bank, the limit on individual withdrawals is half a million yen per transaction, and I can withdraw money several times a day compared to $200 per day in Pittsburgh National Bank's unguarded sidewalk machines. On average, each Japanese machine must hold a great deal more cash than a U.S. machine. Even if the probability of a break-in in Japan is low, the expected loss from break-ins into Japanese machines that hold a lot more money could be higher. If this is the reason for restrictions on hours of ATM operation, banks could install unguarded sidewalk machines open twenty-four hours a day with smaller daily withdrawal limits. Secured machines in supervised bank lobbies could continue to serve for larger withdrawals during restricted hours. Banks have not offered this option.

Employee Opposition

Opposition of bank employees to the introduction of ATMs is understandable. The presence of attendants in ATM lobbies is probably a compromise between management and employees. Bank unions in Kansai (Osaka-Kyoto and vicinity) are said to be weaker than in Kanto (the Tokyo area). Consequently, Osaka-based city banks (Sanwa and Sumitomo) have been most aggressive in banking automation and in trying to expand ATM banking hours.

The textbook story about Japanese industrial organization is that Japan has enterprise unions while the United States has industry unions. Japanese unions are said to protect the viability of the firm, while the U.S. unions insist on their wages and benefits even at the risk of driving some firms into bankruptcy. Would bank employees in Japan insist on retaining obsolete jobs—the featherbedding practices that drove the U.S. railroads into the ground? In Kobe, passengers enter and exit through automated turnstiles at the privately owned Hankyu Rail Line, but the recently (1987) privatized JR lines still use uniformed staff to stamp and take tickets. All six city banks in Japan have long been privately owned (see chapter 25).

If the reluctance to let existing employees go is an important consideration (see chapter 13), one might have expected that the banks would gradually phase in the extra, unmanned ATM hours as their employees retired. But ATM hours have remained frozen, and banks complain of insufficient, not surplus staff. Overstaffing in banks is hardly limited to the ATM lobbies. Compared to U.S. banks, Japanese bank branches have made relatively modest use of computers and software.

Lack of Demand for More Service Hours

Absence of personal need to withdraw cash in the evenings can easily be understood as a statement of habit. Until banks extended their hours to evenings or weekends, and ATMs opened not so long ago, consumers in the United States also arranged their affairs in such a manner that there would be little need to withdraw cash during the hours banks were not open. Of course, U.S. banks offer the convenience of personal checking as well as extensive use of credit cards, substantially reducing the need for cash transactions. Yet, it is in Japan, where cash transactions remain the norm, that ATM technology remains underexploited.

Insufficient Computing Capacity

The insufficient computing capacity explanation for shutting down the ATMs in the evening was given to me by a friend who worked on designing the financial transactions electronic network for Japan's telecommunications company NTT. Though computers are more costly in Japan than in the United States, upon further reflection, considering the low cost of large computing power and the huge Japanese investment in ATM networks, it is difficult to take this explanation seriously.

After-Hours Servicing

Servicing the ATMs during evening and weekend hours hardly requires continuous presence of staff on the spot. ATM technology has matured to a high level of mechanical reliability. Mechanical functioning, cash balance, and even vandalism can be continuously monitored from a centralized remote location that dispatches a mobile service unit. This service function has already been refined to make Japan's vending machine industry the largest in the world (see chapter 17). In any case, the same banks have no difficulty keeping their loan machines open twenty-four hours a day.

Government Regulation

Japanese law does not require banks to obtain permission from the government to change the ATM hours; it only requires them to inform the Ministry of Finance (MOF). Therein lies the rub. In the United States, if there is no specific rule that prohibits some activity, Americans assume that it's okay to go ahead and do it. I was told that in Japan, that was not the case. Japanese banks have to ask formal or informal approval, sometimes called guidance, from the MOF first, even if existing rules and regulations don't specifically prohibit certain activities. If the assumption in Japan is that you can't do it if you don't have permission, it would represent a regulatory philosophy distinct from U.S. practice—you can do it unless it is specifically prohibited.

What Happened in 1978?

The week before I was to return from Japan, a colleague on the Kobe University faculty gave me some old newspaper clippings from *Nikkei Shimbun,* Japan's equivalent of the *Wall Street Journal.* I summarize the stories with their dates in chronological order:

October 3, 1978, Morning Edition, Page 3:
Sumitomo Bank announces that it will extend its ATM hours from 9 A.M.–5 P.M. to 8 A.M.–7 P.M. on weekdays and from 9 A.M.–2 P.M. to 8 A.M.–4 P.M. on Saturdays. Fuji Bank and other city (major) banks are opposed to the idea. It will be costly for them. Sumitomo offers a compromise of a smaller extension. Fuji is still opposed because "it does not add to consumer convenience," and wants the MOF to mediate.

October 19, 1978, Morning Edition, Page 1:
The Antitrust Committee (AC, Japan's equivalent of the U.S. Federal Trade Commission) suspects that the meeting of the six banks about the operating hours of ATMs may have violated the law because such a meeting is unfair restraint of trade used to pressure Sumitomo to change its proposed ATM hours. President of the Bank Association, Mr. Matsuzawa (who is also the head of Fuji Bank), said that the change in operating hours of

ATMs requires the report to the MOF only so that individual banks can decide what is best for them. Neither the Bank Association nor meetings with other banks decide the hours or put pressure on Sumitomo Bank.

October 19, 1978, Evening Edition, Page 1:
The head of the MOF's Bureau of Banking said that, in principle, the decision to change the hours of ATM operation is up to individual financial institutions under the law. We want to make sure that appropriate competition is working among the financial institutions.

October 25, 1978, Morning Edition, Page 3:
Sumitomo Bank extends its ATM hours by fifteen minutes on weekday mornings and by one hour on evenings, leaving the Saturday hours unchanged. The extension is implemented in three metro areas only. President of the Bank Association, Fuji Bank's Mr. Matsuzawa, said that there was no agreement among the banks about this problem. The meeting of the six banks was a regular meeting for the purpose of discussion only, not for deciding anything.

October 29, 1978, Morning Edition, Page 5:
In meetings with the Antitrust Committee the six banks insisted that they did not collude or decide in their meeting of low-level executives who, in any case, do not have the authority to make such decisions. The practice of *gyōsei-shidō* (administrative guidance) from the MOF is appropriate. Banks themselves depend on *gyōsei-shidō* from the MOF. That is, city banks have a strong tradition of *yokonarabi* (level behavior) because they are afraid of too much competition. After the AC's investigation, other banks will follow Sumitomo and extend their hours also. However, people doubt if this new movement will continue in the face of strong *yokonarabi* tradition. In spite of the MOF's announcement about its intent to promote competition, every aspect of banking remains highly regulated. After the shock has passed, things will return to business as usual. The chairmen of the AC are always officials from the MOF or the Bank of Japan. This investigation was unusual in that the AC went into an area that had been sheltered (taboo) before. However, the AC will

not look deeply into *gyōsei-shidō* or *yokonarabi*. The investigation was just a warning against excessive collusion. The MOF publicly insists on an attitude of nonintervention. However, everybody knows that the other banks asked the MOF to stop Sumitomo, and many take it for granted that the MOF played its coordinating role by convincing Sumitomo to cut back on the proposed extension of its ATM hours.

Correspondent's Remark: The MOF's intervention and banks' behavior show that they do not care about customers.

Three years earlier, in 1975, Sanwa Bank had announced twenty-four-hour banking service on its ATMs. The MOF slapped it down because the other city banks, who did not have the technological capability to match it, opposed the plan. Ironically, that opposition was led by Sumitomo Bank.

Government-Managed "Appropriate Competition"

With a few exceptions, ATM hours have remained unchanged. Appropriate competition seems to be a euphemism for tightly controlled competition in Japan's banking industry. Other dimensions of competition are similarly controlled by the MOF. For example, Japan has relatively few but larger bank branches in relationship to the United States. In Japan, unlike in the United States, major banks have a nationwide network of branches. Banks need permission from the MOF to open branches, and the Ministry performs a careful balancing act among the major banks in allowing new branches to be opened. ATMs can be placed only at branches, or within a specified distance from the branches. Consequently, areas with high foot traffic, such as train stations and company cafeterias, have only a few ATMs.

In addition to the operating hours, pricing of ATM services is also of interest. For example, my bank had no charge from 9 A.M. to 6 P.M., charged 103 yen from 6 to 7 P.M., and made it impossible to withdraw cash after 7 P.M. The fee is highest during the hours many office workers leave for home, and may want to stop at the bank to withdraw cash. The fee could be interpreted as a congestion charge during the high-demand hours if the congestion were not the result of limited ATM operating hours. Congestion charges (i.e., higher prices during busy hours) does not seem to be the norm in other sectors of the economy, except on tour packages. Uniformity of the "congestion charge" across banks and cities suggests a centralized origin (such as the Ministry of Finance), or at least an oligopolistic wink-and-nod understanding, rather than a response to local conditions. Today, but not necessarily in the past, different banks, even in the same U.S. city, often set different fees for the same service.

Certain practices reduce effective competition among the major private banks for customer deposits and accounts. Most employers allow employees the choice of only one bank in which they can have their pay deposited directly. Given the absence of personal checking (see chapter 9), it would be quite inconvenient for an employee who is determined to take advantage of the better services of one bank to shift his money from the bank selected by his employer for direct deposit. Most banks don't even try to attract more retail customers by offering better or more convenient services, hours, location, and so on.

In postwar Japan, banks were supposed to support industry by lending to and investing in Japanese corporations. Banks were not interested in providing consumer services—either deposits or loans. This system was enforced by government "window guidance" that allowed banks to borrow from the Bank of Japan at very low interest rates and in turn allowed the banks to lend to businesses at low interest rates. If any bank got out of line, it was "guided" away from the window. Now, the capital control has been lifted and the old system is breaking down, though its remnants linger. Services for bank consumers are still poor (e.g., no personal checking), though they are better than they were a

ATM SLOT MACHINES

decade or two ago. Under "appropriate competition" among major banks, enforced by the MOF, evolution of the whole industry is held down to the rate at which the slowest of the city banks is willing to move.

Why would the government of Japan be a party to this resistance to change? It is possible to argue that a limit on ATM hours, like the absence of personal checking, forces people to carry more cash in their wallets. Since cash is an interest-free loan to the government, it saves about a trillion yen in interest payments on the 37 trillion yen (300,000 yen or 3,000 U.S. dollars per capita) of bank notes in circulation. In comparison, the United States is estimated to have only about $1,000 in bank notes in circulation per capita and, unlike Japan's, more than half of U.S. currency is believed to be held outside the United States.

It is difficult to apportion the responsibility between the banks and the government. Whoever is to blame, the result is that the price of ATM transactions is zero during working hours, 103 yen in the most popular time slot after work, and rises to a priceless infinity after that.

20

Why Is Rice So Expensive in Japan?

Susumu Hondai

The Japanese written character for "rice" *(gohan)* is the same as for "food." Surprisingly, this staple of the Japanese diet is far more expensive in Japan than in the rest of the world. In 1995, the producer and retail prices of rice in Japan were 9.4 and 3.4 times the respective prices in the United States. In February 1996, 10 kilograms (22 pounds) of high-quality nonglutinous rice sold at an average retail price of 5,585 yen, or, roughly 56 U.S. dollars. That price was two and a half times as expensive as the ultrapremium short-grain rice sold in Honolulu at the time. Why is rice so expensive in Japan?

Historical Significance of Rice

Rice is by far the most important agricultural product in Japan. Nevertheless, the share of rice in Japan's agricultural production has declined from 60 percent at the time of the Meiji Restoration (1868) to about 30 percent today. Rice culture in Japan is suitable and profitable as a crop for part-time farmers, who cultivate small plots of land, currently averaging about 1.65 acres. Rice cultivation and its attendant rituals form the base of many of the festivities and cultural artifacts that give the Japanese their sense of identity. Rice is also regarded as basic to Japan's national security. The government has used these reasons to pursue a policy of rice self-sufficiency.

This policy lies at the heart of the high price of rice in Japan. To understand this policy, it is necessary to look first at the Food Control Act of 1942 and at some of the modifications to that Act up until the 1994 Amendment.

The Food Control Act of 1942

In response to the food shortages and high prices of World War II, the Food Control Act of 1942 imposed strict control over the rice market. The Japanese government took sole charge of all rice production, distribution, and sales and since then has maintained substantial control or influence over all areas. Though the Act has been modified several times since 1942, its basic premise of supplying rice to consumers at a stable price through direct government intervention remains in force today.

To accomplish the objective of an adequate supply of rice at stable prices, the government controlled rice marketing by regulating both producer and consumer prices as well as rice imports. Traders had to obtain permission from the Japanese Food Agency to import or export rice. This control enabled the Agency to insulate the domestic rice market from the world market. Between 1970 and 1994, almost no rice was imported into Japan except for small quantities of rice flour and various kinds of special-purpose rice such as mochi-rice (glutinous rice used for making cakes), cracked rice, and Thai rice (which is used for making *awamori*, distilled rice spirits produced in Okinawa).

The government did not directly control rice production, in terms of setting limits on how much land rice farmers could till, until 1971. Since then, each farmer has been allotted a quota of rice land, thereby limiting the total amount of rice produced each year.

Setting the Price of Rice

Rice is "collected" from the farmers by producer cooperatives or rice merchants. Under the Staple Food Act of 1942, all rice collectors, wholesalers, and retailers had to be licensed by the government. Until 1969, all rice produced had to be sold to the government. The Japanese Food Agency would buy rice at a pre-determined price set each year after consultation with the Rice Price Advisory Council. Since 1960, this government-purchase price has been set in accordance with the cost of production and to provide the rice growers with a standard of living comparable to that of urban workers. After purchase, the Japanese Food Agency then sells the rice to wholesalers at prices set by the government. Since 1972, the government has also announced a sug-gested retail price for rice. Although the government now has no direct control over the retail price, in actual practice, the re-tail price for rice rarely deviates much from the suggested price.

In 1969, the government introduced a voluntary marketing system to provide farmers with an additional market in which to sell rice. Rice marketed under the voluntary marketing system did not qualify for government price support. The price was de-termined through negotiation between agricultural coopera-tives representing the rice growers and rice wholesalers.

One reason for the introduction of this voluntary system was to cut the government's cost of providing price supports. In the absence of fixed prices in this market, farmers prefer to sell their better-quality rice in this market rather than to the gov-ernment's Food Agency. Consequently, voluntarily marketed rice receives a price premium of about 25 percent at the whole-sale level and 35 percent at the retail level over government-marketed rice. As a consequence of these changes, the amount of rice sold to the government decreased. In 1990, about 30 percent of produced rice was sold to the Japanese Food Agency as *government-marketed rice*. The remaining 70 percent was sold to the National Federation of Agricultural Cooperative Associa-tions (Zennō) as *voluntarily-marketed rice*.

Effects of Price and Output Regulation

During the 1960s, when Japan still faced food shortages, the government introduced rice rationing and kept the retail price of rice low. Rice is an inferior good in Japan in that people want to buy less rice when their incomes rise. With increasing economic prosperity in Japan, per capita consumption of rice has declined continuously, dropping from an annual 111.7 kilograms in 1965 to 66 kilograms in 1994. As a result of this decrease in consumption, along with increase in income, the share of the average family's food budget spent on rice has dropped to about 5 percent in spite of the high price of rice. (By contrast, the Japanese presently eat 6 times as much meat, 4 times as much milk and dairy products, and 2 times as much fruit as they did in 1960.)

The price support program did not permit the price of rice to drop with demand. The retail price was kept high, and farmers were often paid even more than the retail price, the difference coming as a subsidy from the government treasury. Because there is no direct link between producer and consumer prices, labor unions in Japan have historically supported high producer prices even as they demanded low consumer prices.

As demand for rice continued to decline, the cost of the rice price support program became unbearably large for the government. To reduce the financial drain on the treasury, the government introduced a land set-aside program, in which growers were required to leave some of their land untilled in order to bring supply in line with demand. Under the Rice Production Control and Diversion Program, the central government sets a nationwide target for rice production based on estimated demand for each year. Land set-aside targets are then allocated by the central government among the prefectures on the basis of past government purchases, annual rice production, and other considerations. It is now up to each prefectural government to distribute the set-aside target among the farmers in its area.

Why Don't Consumers Complain?

Japan's pro-farmer policies that keep domestic food prices high were understandable as long as farmers dominated Japanese national politics. However, Japan's rapid economic growth after World War II induced massive population migration from the rural areas into the cities. Although as recently as 1960, 80 percent of the political districts were rural districts, farm households now represent about 8 percent of the nation's households and 10 percent of the total population, and less than one-fifth of those households farm full-time. The benefits of agricultural protection therefore flow only to a small percentage of the Japanese population. Why don't the growing legion of urban consumers complain about high food prices?

Since expenditures on rice now represent less than 2 percent of the average household budget, the effect of the high price of rice on the cost of living is insignificant. As a result, Japanese consumers have not complained about its high price. (On the other hand, rice producers outside Japan look at the high price of rice and the large rice-consuming population, and they have become vociferous in their complaints about Japan's closed rice market.) While many Japanese recognize the overall economic benefits of a freer trade regime, those benefits are also likely to be spread thinly among the large number of consumers, businesses, and trade unions. Thus, no interest group has successfully challenged the farm lobby's defense of Japan's protectionist agricultural policy.

Rice Marketing under the Amendment of 1994

The 1994 Amendment to the Food Control Act of 1942 represents another revision of Japan's rice policy. The principal changes are as follows. (1) The government no longer requires farmers to sell their rice to the government. Thus most rice will

Once upon a time there was a child named Pandora-chan who was desperate for a rice ball...

now be marketed voluntarily without price controls. Government rice purchase is limited to 1.5 million tons per year. (2) The acreage allotment program applies only to growers who want to sell rice to the government. (3) Instead of allowing government-held stocks of rice to rise, the government intends to announce fixed targets for rice stocks. (4) Under the recently concluded Uruguay Round of General Agreement on Tariff and Trade (GATT), Japan has agreed to import limited amounts of rice each year or a total of 3.6 million tons between 1995 and 2000. (5) The government now allows anyone to sell rice.

Will the Price of Rice Decrease?

In the first several months after the implementation of the Amendment in 1995, the retail price of rice fell by 20 percent. In 1995, the government imported 380,000 tons of rice and will increase imports gradually to 760,000 tons by the year 2000. This, however, amounts to a mere 7 percent of domestic rice consumption, and is not large enough to bring the price of rice in Japan down to the international level. Moreover, the Amendment still gives authority to the Japanese Food Agency to restrict rice production. Although the Amendment states that acreage allotments would apply only to farmers who plan to sell rice to the government, the Agency plans to impose planting restrictions on most growers for the foreseeable future.

Japan's protectionist policies toward farmers are definitely changing. With redistricting, political power in Japan is shifting from farmers and small businesses to urban consumers and large corporations. Pressure from the United States and Japan's other trading partners to open Japan to agricultural imports has also weakened the farmers' cause. Internally, Japanese corporations that have large stakes in overseas markets have also increasingly urged the ruling political party in Japan (the Liberal Democratic Party) to reduce its protection of agriculture. The price of rice in Japan may therefore fall farther in the future, but the Japanese won't be eating inexpensive rice any time soon.

21

How Can the Japanese Spend So Little on Health Care?

Matthew Loke and James Mak

Many Americans are unhappy with the U.S. health care system but they do not agree on how it should be reformed. Americans cherish their personal choice of high-quality health care but are unhappy with unequal access and soaring costs. The Clinton administration's effort in 1994 to get Congress to pass its health care bill generated heated political debate but little action. Cost of medical care in the United States rises at the fastest rate among industrialized countries. Yet, 15 percent of Americans, including 10 million children, have no health insurance.

By contrast, everyone in Japan is covered by health insurance. Japan also has much lower health care expenditures per person. The Paris-based Organization for Economic Co-operation and Development (OECD) calculates that in 1994 Japan spent 1,473 U.S. dollars per person on health care compared to 3,516 U.S. dollars per person in the United States. Japan spent about 7 percent of its gross domestic product on health care compared to 14 percent for the United States. Compared to other Western industrialized countries, Japan's expenditures on health care, whether per person or as a percentage of the country's gross domestic product, are not particularly low. It is the United States that is the exceptionally big spender on health care.

Japan's health care system is designed to achieve two goals: (1) universal access to health care, and (2) direct government control of health care expenditures. Two-thirds of the medical costs in Japan are public, not private expenditures.

Universal Access to Health Care

Japan's health care financing system is based on a social insurance model patterned after the German health care system but with more direct government intervention. Everyone is covered by one of three types of plan and, by law, no one can opt out of the system. Over 62 percent of the population are covered by 1,800 employer plans. These plans are designed for employees and their dependents, with premiums equally shared between employers and employees. Premiums are automatically deducted from the payroll as part of the employee's social security system contributions. Employees' twice-per-year bonuses (see chapter 14) are not subject to premium deductions. Total premiums typically amount to less than 3 percent of the employee's total income, including bonuses. Co-payments—the part of the medical bills that employees have to pay—range from 10 to 30 percent, and help keep frivolous expenditures down.

Medical care benefits covered under employee health insurance plans are established by law and include almost all inpatient and outpatient treatments. However, coverage does not include preventive health care measures such as immunizations, annual physicals, and lab tests (urinalysis, serum cholesterol). Delivery of a baby (without complications) is also excluded, since it is not regarded as an illness.

Local governments and trade associations offer a second type of health plan for the self-employed, pensioners, and their dependents. Premiums are based on income and assets and the number of persons covered. Since people insured under this system generally have lower incomes and are at higher medical risk, the national government provides a direct subsidy to the insurers. The elderly are also covered by this plan unless they are employed or their (low) income level allows them to be covered under their children's plans as dependents. The co-payment rate under this plan is 30 percent. Until recently co-payment was waived for the elderly, enabling them to obtain free medical care. This arrangement had to be abandoned due to soaring costs. The elderly now have to pay 10 percent of the total fee. Most of the cost of geriatric care is paid out of a fund that receives contributions from the two insurance systems as well as subsidies from the national and local governments.

Under both plans there is a cap on the total amount of monthly medical expenditures that the insured can be asked to pay. On average, individuals pay about 12 percent of their total medical bills directly; the balance is paid by insurance plans and government subsidies.

Finally, there is also a separate plan for people on welfare (i.e., public assistance) that covers less than one percent of the population. Private health insurance is available in Japan but only as supplementary coverage.

In the United States, medical insurance under fee-for-service plans usually has a lifetime maximum on medical expenses. When the maximum amount is reached, members are subject to an annual renewable benefit. By contrast, there is no lifetime spending cap on medical insurance coverage in Japan.

Low-cost Health Care

The reason Japan spends less than the United States on health care is not because the Japanese consult their doctors less often or have shorter hospital stays. Quite the contrary. For every out-patient visit of an American, a Japanese makes three visits. And the average inpatient hospital stay for a Japanese is 8 times that of his or her American counterpart (forty-eight days versus six days in 1993). Also, except for hospital beds, there are no restrictions imposed on other forms of capital investments such as those imposed on high-tech equipment in the United States.

The government of Japan maintains tight control over prices on virtually all health care services. Payments to medical care providers are made on a fee-for-service basis, which most health care economists agree does not provide an incentive to contain costs. Health care costs in Japan have been contained by a national detailed fee schedule that sets uniform fees for every service for all health care providers regardless of their experience, reputation, or location. Each medical service is assigned a specific number of points, and each point is worth 10 yen.

The fee for each service is inclusive and covers all supplies and materials, capital depreciation, and personnel costs, including physician and surgeon fees. Given uniform fees for a particular service, patients—with few exceptions—cannot negotiate with their doctors and hospitals to get higher-quality service. Extra charges are permitted only for private hospital rooms and the use of a very restricted range of new technology. Not surprisingly, medical service providers don't have the incentive to provide high-quality service. A special council (Central Social Insurance Medical Council) within the Ministry of Health and Welfare oversees revisions to the fee schedule; the council is comprised of eight providers, eight payers, and four consumers who represent the public.

By changing the fee schedule, the Ministry of Health and Welfare influences the allocation of medical services provided. For example, by constraining fees for surgical services, the Ministry has kept surgical rates low, thus allowing it to directly control expenditures for medical care.

Price, Quantity, Quality, and Value of Time

Price and quality control over health care services define the incentive structure facing providers and patients and yield predictable results. Physicians are required by law to accept as payment in full the fees set under the uniform fee schedule. Because of their low fees per consultation, physicians have the incentive to see many patients for brief consultations. For a given episode of illness, Japanese patients are likely to make multiple visits to their physician, whereas in the United States only a single visit might suffice. In effect, since government fixes the price of a visit, physicians simply adjust the quantity of service they deliver in a single visit to suit their goals.

The physician fee schedule also favors ambulatory service in clinics over inpatient hospital care. Also, surgical procedures in hospitals are reimbursed a flat fee without any consideration for case severity or the amount of surgeon's time required. Since all hospital surgeons are salaried staff, there is little incentive to perform surgery unless absolutely necessary. This incentive structure partly explains the much lower hospital admission rates and incidence of surgical procedures in Japan compared to that in the United States.

An apparent paradox exists with the much higher average length of stay in Japanese hospitals (forty-eight days compared to six days in the United States) and the number of hospital beds (sixteen beds per thousand population compared to slightly over four in the United States). A great part of this discrepancy exists because Japanese hospital beds are substitutes for long-term nursing home beds, and the data do not differentiate between acute-care and long-term care facilities. The Ministry of Health and Welfare estimates that 45 percent of all hospital inpatients are elderly individuals (age sixty-five and over) at any given time and over half of these patients have been hospitalized for more than three months. Unlike in the United States, nursing homes are not common in Japan because, in part, they are viewed as places where uncaring children abandon their elderly parents. Perhaps, more important, it is not easy to be admitted into public nursing homes. For example, admission into the "special nursing home for the elderly" (tokubetsu yōgo rōjin hōmu) is decided by the local government, and admission is granted only to those who are bedridden and whose mental and physical disabilities are so severe that they require constant care *and* it is not possible to receive the required care at home. Thus, someone with a spouse, child, or child-in-law who could care for him or her at home might be denied admission into the nursing home. The rich can enter commercial nursing homes, which may require an admission fee of 50 to 100 million yen (500,000 to 1 million U.S. dollars) plus a monthly fee of 200,000 to 300,000 yen (2,000 to 3,000 U.S. dollars). Not surprisingly, hospitals are widely used as nursing homes, increasing Japan's hospital bed capacity and the average length of hospital stay. Nonetheless, hospital stays in Japan are significantly longer than in the United States, even after accounting for patient and case mix.

Since Japan's hospital admission rate is half that of the United States, its hospital bed occupancy rate is also lower. Under such circumstances, hospital physicians in Japan have more discretion in extending patient length of stay in hospitals. In the absence of reimbursement limits by insurers, hospitals could also generate more revenue by filling up the empty beds. This is reinforced by Japan's medical tradition of emphasizing bed rest and pampering the sick.

In sum, while the uniform fee schedule has been able to contain the per unit cost of medical services delivered, it has not been able to limit the quantity of services and specify the quality of services consumed. This loophole reduces the effect the government price controls might have in containing the cost of health care. Nonetheless, out-of-pocket medical care costs in Japan are lower in part because Japanese hospitals provide less intensive services, and patients rely on family members to provide a substantial amount of the nursing services in the hospitals.

In addition to out-of-pocket costs, time costs should also be considered. Government price controls say nothing about time. Consequently, convenience and delay in timing of medical services is the second important way in which the laws of economics function in Japanese health care in spite of government price control. Multiple short visits to the physician's office are costly to patients. Further, patients are not given appointments and typically have to wait for an hour or more at physicians' offices or hospitals. Thus the real cost of health care in Japan is much higher than indicated by government statistics since official data include only the cash costs but not the higher cost of travel and waiting time Japanese patients face. Additionally, physicians in Japan customarily receive large sums of money as "monetary gifts" from their patients as expressions of gratitude (see chapter 4). These payments, tax-free to physicians, are also not included in Japanese medical expenditure data, again understating Japanese health care costs. The Japanese health care system also encourages doctors to prescribe large quantities of medicine (see chapter 18).

Although prices of medical services are uniform across providers, quality dispensed is not. Predictably, when the cash price is prevented from serving its allocative function in the economy, the noncash price—multiple visits, travel, and waiting time in this case—takes over. Quality providers such as university and large public hospitals have long lines of patients. These patients cannot be turned away because the system, as in the United States, is designed to allow patients the free choice of health care providers. Wealthy patients can trade off money for time and buy high-quality medical care abroad. For instance, some wealthy Japanese patients travel to Hawaii to have open heart surgery performed by a famous Japanese-American surgeon who is known to meet his patients personally at the Honolulu International Airport in a limousine. A comparative study of patient satisfaction at two medical sites in Japan and two sites in the United States (all university-affiliated teaching hospitals) in the fall of 1991 found that Americans were generally more satisfied with their medical care than their Japanese counterparts.

Health care providers on the two sides of the Pacific Ocean may have different opinions about the relative quality of health care services in the two countries. Statistics show that Japan has better health indexes. Japanese have the longest life expectancy

(at birth) and the lowest infant mortality of any industrialized country. However, Japan's impressive health indexes might not be explained by the quality of its health care system; instead they may help explain why per capita cash expenditures on health care are so much lower than in the United States. Healthy people spend less on medical care. Exactly why Japan has such impressive health indicators is still being researched; a leading explanation is the Japanese low-fat diet. Some people believe that the Shinto religion, which emphasizes personal cleanliness thus avoiding contamination, and Chinese medical influence, which emphasizes preventive care, also help keep the Japanese healthy. Few AIDS cases and a much lower incidence of drug abuse and violent crime also contribute to Japan's lower per capita cash expenditures on medical care. Relative infrequency of medical malpractice suits against physicians and hospitals further help reduce the need to practice defensive medicine and thus lower medical expenditures.

The Rising Cost of Medical Care

The Japanese people presently enjoy universal access to health care at relatively low cash cost but high time cost. Even the cash cost advantage may not last for long. Potentially, the most important factor influencing future health care expenditures in Japan is the rapidly aging population. By the year 2010, 21.3 percent of the Japanese population is expected to be age sixty-five or over, compared to 12.9 percent for the United States. Japan's aging population will demand more medical care services and more long-term care facilities. Medical expenditures for an elderly person are 5 times higher than for a young person. Japan's aging population will place severe strains on the nation's health care financing system.

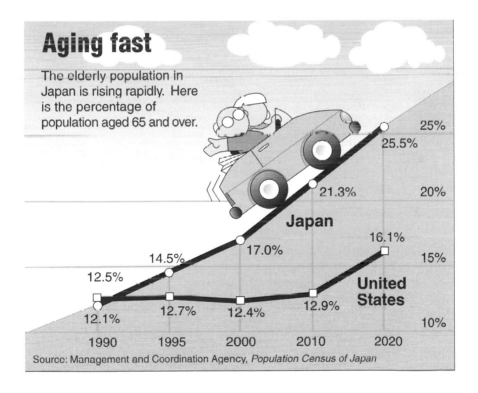

Aging fast

The elderly population in Japan is rising rapidly. Here is the percentage of population aged 65 and over.

25%

25.5%

20%

21.3%

Japan

16.1%

17.0%

15%

14.5%

12.5%

United States

12.7%   12.4%   12.9%

12.1%

10%

1990   1995   2000   2010   2020

Source: Management and Coordination Agency, *Population Census of Japan*

22

How Does Japan's Largest Bank Work?

Toshiki Jinushi

According to *Fortune* magazine, the three largest banks in the world in 1995 were Dai-Ichi-Kangyo, Tokyo-Mitsubishi, and Sakura. Not many outside Japan know of an even bigger bank—the Japanese Postal Savings Office (PSO). With its deposits of over 200 trillion yen (2 trillion U.S. dollars) in mid-1995, PSO is much larger than the three largest banks in the world combined. And its share of Japanese deposits has been rising.

The PSO has 24,500 branches throughout Japan. Being part of the Japanese Ministry of Posts and Telecommunications, every post office in the country doubles as a branch of this bank. In contrast, even the largest of the commercial banks have only six or seven hundred branches. The ten largest commercial banks and the sixty-four regional banks in Japan have 19,000 branches combined. In rural areas, the PSO has little competition. But why have the commercial banks not driven it out of business in the urban areas, where most Japanese live today? On the contrary, starting from about 10 percent of deposits in the early 1960s, the PSO was able to account for about 45 percent of deposits in 1996.

Popularity of the Postal Savings Office

Since the PSO is backed by the full faith and credit of the government of Japan, depositors prefer to keep their money in the PSO, especially during times of economic uncertainty. Until quite recently, the PSO consistently paid higher interest rates on deposits than the commercial banks. Lower risk and higher return is an unbeatable combination in investment markets. In addition, the PSO enjoys great economies of scale; it also doesn't have to pay taxes, stamp duties, or deposit insurance, and is able to offer products and services commercial banks cannot match. Its "fixed amount deposits" (*teigaku* deposit certificates), for example, pay a higher rate of return and provide greater liquidity than the time deposits offered by private commercial banks. Fixed-amount deposits are long-term savings deposits in standard denominations (e.g., 10,000 yen denominations) with ten-year maturities, but can be withdrawn with only a minor penalty six months after the date of deposit. Because of their popularity, fixed-amount deposits now account for almost 90 percent of the postal savings deposits. Until recently, commercial banks were barred from offering a similar product. By contrast, term deposits offered by commercial banks were limited to a maximum maturity of only two years, and they offered lower interest rates. Some commercial banks and credit unions recently announced plans to offer a term deposit similar to that offered by PSO, but it will take time for them to erode PSO's dominant market share.

Another reason for the large size of the PSO is that it does not compete with the commercial banks on a level playing field. Indeed, it holds the upper hand. The Ministry of Posts and Telecommunications, of which the PSO is a part, eagerly encourages innovation by the PSO to expand and improve services to its depositors. The PSO is regarded as the most depositor-oriented bank in Japan. It charges no fees for use of its automatic teller machines outside the normal business hours, and offers the lowest-cost money transfer service (which is especially valuable in Japan, where there are no personal checking accounts; see chapter 9). The high efficiency of its three main services—mail, deposits, and insurance—can be attributed to its ability to share the cost of facilities and staff among the three services.

On the other hand, the Ministry of Finance, which regulates the commercial banks, emphasizes the stability of the financial markets as its primary goal. The Ministry of Finance has tried hard to stifle competition among the commercial banks by its sluggishness in permitting them to introduce new products. As a result, commercial banks have functioned under cartel-like coordination to the disadvantage of their depositors. The presence of the PSO helps limit the monopoly power and cartel-like behavior of the commercial banks.

Where Does the Money Go?

The PSO takes deposits but, in principle, it does not make loans. Instead, it turns over almost all of its funds—deposits as well as insurance premiums—to the Fund Management Bureau of the Ministry of Finance for investment. Not being an incorporated full-service bank, it doesn't appear at the top of *Fortune*'s list of largest banks in the world.

Managing 45 percent of total bank deposits in Japan is an enormous task. The efficiency with which the huge fund of deposits and insurance premiums are collected is only matched by the amazing inefficiency in their investment. The fund is so large that it is appropriately called the "Second National Budget." During the postwar high-growth phase of the Japanese economy, money in the fund was used mainly for public investments and loans. These disbursements are susceptible to political influence. Basically, funds are allocated among various sectors, such as agriculture, public housing, individual housing loans, small business, and regional development, with each getting virtually a fixed share. Even as the Japanese economy is deregulated, allocation of these funds remains substantially under the pressure of vested interests, and has come under increasing criticism.

The Fund Management Bureau itself has only a small staff. A dozen public corporations, such as the Public Housing Loan Corporation, North-East Regional Development Corporation, Export-Import Bank, and Public Small-Business Loan Corporation, channel the funds into various investments and loans.

For instance, let us look at how the Public Housing Loan Corporation (PHLC) works. If you want to build a house for yourself for the first time in Japan, you can borrow most of the necessary funds from the PHLC. You can go to any branch of a commercial bank and the clerk will show you how much you can borrow from the PHLC and how much you need to borrow from the commercial bank, and will fill in all the necessary application forms. You would borrow the maximum permissible amount from the PHLC because it is a subsidized (i.e., below-market) mortgage loan. The PHLC's loan rates are even lower than the interest rate the Postal Savings Office pays to its depositors. In effect, the PHLC borrows funds from the PSO through the Fund Management Bureau; the difference in interest rates between what PSO pays to its depositors and the PHLC charges for its loans is subsidized by the Ministry of Construction, which gets its money from the national budget.

The Future of the Postal Savings Office

The "Second National Budget" played an important role during Japan's postwar high-growth era. While the commercial banks financed large private business investments, the PSO mobilized funds to finance investments in public infrastructure, housing, and small businesses. As the first round of public infrastructure development now comes to an end, and as the large businesses cut back their dependence on bank loans, the role of the "Second National Budget" is being reexamined. Today, only about 20 percent of the money that the PSO takes in goes into public investment. The rest is being used to make loans to private companies, thus competing directly with commercial bank lending, and to buy securities. At the same time, commercial banks are moving into nonbusiness financing that they neglected during the high-growth era. A growing number of critics are calling for the government to reestablish the PSO as a private bank.

23

Why Do So Many Japanese Contribute to Public TV?

Kazuhiro Igawa and James Mak

In Japan, public radio and television broadcasts are provided by a semipublic monopoly popularly known as NHK (Nihon Hoso Kyokai), the Japan Broadcasting Corporation. As in public broadcasting in the United States, NHK does not air commercials and thus receives no revenue from that source. But NHK and public television in the United States have some important differences, one of the most striking being the difference in funding base.

Financing Public Broadcasting in the United States

There are over 400 independent public radio stations and about 350 local public television stations in the United States. Funding for public broadcasting comes largely from government subsidies, corporate and charitable foundation underwriting grants, and, to a lesser degree, from voluntary listener and viewer contributions. Few people who watch public television or listen to public radio contribute directly to the production and distribution of the programs. For instance, Hawaii Public Radio (KHPR) notes in its annual fund drives that only 10 percent of the listeners contribute to KHPR. Its television counterpart, Hawaii Public Television (KHET), reports that about 50 percent of the Hawaii households with television sets tune into KHET programming, but viewer contributions comprise only 13 percent of KHET's total annual revenues. Nationally, only about 10 percent of the viewers of public television actually contribute directly to their local station's operating budget. Economists who study people's behavior in voluntary giving are not surprised by the low rate of individual contributions, since those who refuse to pay can still receive public broadcasts. Thus, most of the people who enjoy public broadcasting contribute nothing directly to their production and distribution and instead hope that others will contribute enough to keep their favorite programs on the air. Public broadcasting in the United States is chronically underfunded.

Paying for NHK

As with the more famous British Broadcasting Corporation (BBC), NHK is not a national broadcasting agency and receives no operating money from the national government treasury. NHK is a public service broadcasting organization that gets its funding from receivers' fees. It gets government help in the form of a law that empowers it to collect receiver fees to pay for its expenses. NHK began in 1953 with only 866 reception contracts. In fiscal year 1995, NHK had total revenues of 570 billion yen, of which 554 billion yen (97 percent) were raised through more than 35 million user "contracts" or receiver fees.

Bill collectors fan out across the country every two months, visiting individual homes to assess and collect fees from those who own television sets. Although national legislation requires that owners of television sets pay the fees subject to a penalty equal to twice the normal fee, the law is not strictly enforced. Before television sets became widely owned (today, 99 percent of households have at least one TV), fees were collected only on the ownership of radio sets. Fees were discontinued on radio sets in 1968, the year that NHK began assessing owners for color televisions. The size of the fee depends on the kind of television set owned. For instance a family that owns a color television set has to pay a monthly fee of 1,370 yen (about 13 U.S. dollars), and 2,300 yen per month if the family owns a color television set that can receive satellite transmissions. The fee for a black-and-white television set is lower than that for a color set, 890 yen per month. The average monthly fee in 1995–1996 was about 1,320 yen, suggesting that households do their best to contract for the lowest possible rate.

In principle, NHK charges a fee for each television set, but in actual practice only a single fee is collected per household regardless of the number of television sets owned. (This does not apply to institutions.) The size of the fee also depends on whether it is collected in person or sent in through electronic bank transfer. Since fees are discounted if they are paid through bank transfers, most households (over 80 percent) today pay them electronically rather than to collectors. To publicly identify those households that have paid their fees, an NHK tag is affixed to the street entrance of the residence.

Many people also pay because they get many direct benefits from NHK broadcasts. Unlike public broadcasting in the United States, NHK competes directly with private, commercial television networks in many programming areas. In the area of television news, NHK has no peer. Despite the fact that Japan publishes more daily newspapers per capita than any of the Western industrialized countries, the Japanese are far more dependent on television than printed news, and NHK is the most important and trusted source of television news in Japan. Indeed, surveys in the late 1970s found that NHK was the most trusted institution in Japanese society.

Nonpayers

Legislation requiring people to pay the user fee combined with door-to-door collection reduces, but does not eliminate, the number of nonpayers. However, the nonpayer may suffer social disapproval from neighbors who have tags on their own doors. Second, some people refuse to pay, claiming that they don't watch NHK programming, and some won't pay because they believe that NHK reporting is biased in favor of the government. Third, some people grudgingly pay less than the full fee by offering to pay the lower fee for a black-and-white television instead of the higher fee for a color television (collectors do not usually enter their homes to check), or they pay only when the collector aggressively pursues collection.

Putting on the Pressure

Fee collectors use a variety of strategies to get people to pay. To refute those who say they don't watch NHK television broadcasting, collectors may show up during the NHK broadcasts of the popular Japanese wrestling *(sumō)* tournaments. (NHK has a monopoly on the broadcast of *sumō* tournaments!) Collectors sometimes use electronic devices to check for the presence of television sets. When a family offers reasons for not paying, a collector may argue with the homeowner using a very loud voice so that neighbors can hear. Many housewives are intimidated by the aggressive collectors, and to avoid personal confrontation, they elect to pay the fees regularly through automatic electronic bank transfers.

The zeal and persistence of NHK in collecting user fees was personally experienced by one of the authors. In December 1996, Professor Igawa rebuilt his house in Kobe after it had been destroyed by the January 1995 Great Hanshin Earthquake; within a week of its completion, an NHK collector showed up at the house to collect the receiver fee. (How did he know the house was rebuilt?) Then, in January 1997, the family added an antenna to receive satellite TV transmissions. The following month, NHK sent them a higher bill for owning a satellite dish.

According to NHK, nearly 85 percent of the households with television sets in Japan have contracts to pay receiver fees. Our own calculation suggests the number may be less than 80 percent. Nevertheless, NHK has a remarkably high subscription rate.

High Cost of Collection

The cost of collection is high. For fiscal year 1995, NHK spent 75 billion yen to collect 554 billion yen in user fees, or a collection cost-to-revenue ratio of 13.5 percent. Since just about every household in Japan owns at least one television set, wouldn't it be more efficient to scrap this costly collection system, and instead raise everybody's taxes just a little bit and use general tax revenues to fund public broadcasting? The answer is a definite "yes." The ratio of administrative costs to total tax revenues collected in Japan has been declining since the late 1970s and is less than one percent today.

The disadvantage of using tax financing is the public concern that NHK might lose its independence to the government. While its board of governors is appointed by the prime minister and its yearly budget must be approved by the Ministry of Posts and the national legislature (the Diet), the government presently does not have control over NHK's day-to-day administration.

24

Why Are So Few People on Welfare in Japan?

Yoko Kimura

In January 1995, the Great Hanshin Earthquake struck Kobe City and the surrounding areas, killing more than six thousand people and making more than three hundred thousand people homeless. Yet news reporters covering the disaster noted that large numbers of households that qualified for disaster relief refused to apply for public assistance. Why are the Japanese reluctant to seek public assistance?

Japan imposes stringent qualification rules on welfare recipients. In 1995, while still caught in the grips of the country's worst and longest economic recession since World War II, less than 1.5 percent of all households and 0.7 percent of the population in Japan received general welfare assistance. The percentage of Japanese households receiving welfare assistance has declined from 2.3 percent in 1965 and 2.0 percent in 1985.

Japan's welfare system is designed to discourage able-bodied individuals from receiving public assistance. In 1995, 84.1 percent of the households receiving public assistance were either elderly or sick or handicapped households, and only 8.8 percent were single-parent households headed by women with dependent children

U.S. Welfare Dependency

In contrast to Japan's low welfare dependency, in 1993, 8.6 percent of American households received cash public assistance; 9.4 percent of the households received food stamps; 5.3 percent received housing assistance; and 13.5 percent received medical care assistance through the Medicaid program. In 1992, 13.5 percent of the U.S. population participated in at least one major means-tested public assistance program. Strikingly, 49.0 percent of the population in families with female head of household (no spouse present) and related children under eighteen years of age received at least one type of major means-tested welfare assistance. In that year, the United States spent an equivalent of 3.5 percent of the gross domestic product on welfare assistance, compared to only 0.3 percent in Japan. Rising welfare dependency has become a social problem of great concern to Americans, prompting the U.S. Congress and the Clinton administration to pass a landmark welfare reform bill in 1996 that would drastically curtail public assistance benefits and eligibility in America.

Who Qualifies to Receive Welfare Assistance in Japan?

In Japan, households, not individuals, qualify for welfare assistance. By contrast, in the United States, welfare eligibility focuses on the individual. Japanese law does not precisely define who is poor, granting some discretion to the local government, even the individual social worker, in deciding who qualifies for welfare assistance. As a rule of thumb, assistance is given to bring the recipient's income up to 60 percent of the average income of laborers. Assets, such as home equity, are converted into income streams and included in the calculation.

Qualifying households can receive cash assistance to pay for food and clothing, housing, compulsory education (including school lunch), funeral costs, maternity costs, and job-related (e.g., job training) costs. They can also obtain free medical care. About three-quarters of the cost of welfare assistance is paid by the national government; local governments administer the programs and pay the other 25 percent.

Reasons for Low Welfare Dependency

Why is the welfare dependency ratio lower in Japan? Japan's fast economic growth after World War II produced low unemployment rates, high wages, and hence fewer poor people (see chapter 26). Japan also has one of the most equal distributions of income among developed countries. Improving social security benefits means that fewer elderly people need financial assistance.

The design of Japan's welfare system also keeps dependency low. The law stipulates that a household cannot qualify for welfare assistance if its members have direct (lineal) blood relatives (or, if there is a relative living with them) who can provide financial support. Lineal blood relatives include parents, children, and siblings. Sometimes family courts determine which relatives must provide financial support for needy family members. By tradition, Japanese children were expected to care for their elderly parents. In a Japanese family the eldest son and his wife often live with his parents and are expected to provide financial support as well as personal care. More than 60 percent of the Japanese elderly live with their extended families. Since husbands and wives are not blood relatives, the law further stipulates that spouses must support each other. In sum, Japan places the financial burden of supporting the poor on the family. The government provides help only as a last resort.

Social values also keep welfare dependency low. Hard work and high propensity to save are considered personal and social virtues by the Japanese. (Chapter III, Article 27 of the Japanese Constitution states that "all people shall have the right and the *obligation* to work.") Being poor in Japan is looked

on as evidence of lack of personal effort and brings shame to the family and relatives. Applying for welfare benefits brings invasion of privacy, intimidation, and humiliation. Applicants are investigated thoroughly for all potential sources of income; neighbors are questioned; and applicants are asked many personal questions about family relationships (e.g., Where is your son? How much money does he make? etc.). The government monitors welfare recipients very closely. The *Asahi Shimbun,* one of the two largest-circulation newspapers in Japan, recently reported the story of a family whose welfare assistance was cut off because it had set aside a small amount of money for funeral expenses. The government's response was that the family could apply for aid to pay for funerals. Many poor households do not apply for welfare assistance because of the shame associated with receiving public aid.

What Is the Future of Welfare?

The reluctance of the Japanese to apply for welfare assistance suggests that the number of poor households in Japan may be larger than the official welfare assistance statistics indicate. Some people who need financial assistance don't get the necessary help because they are ashamed either to apply for public assistance or to ask relatives for help. The good points of the Japanese welfare system are that it does not encourage individuals to quit work in order to collect welfare. Nor does it encourage men to abandon their families.

Whether Japan will continue to enjoy low welfare dependency in the future is a big question. The number of elderly households in Japan is rising rapidly. Before World War II, 40 percent of the Japanese families had three generations living together; today the nuclear family is more common. The number of elderly people living on their own is rising rapidly, and many don't expect their adult children to provide them with financial support and long-term personal care. The Japanese also appear to be less reluctant to apply for public assistance. These indicators, combined with slower expected economic growth in the future, suggest that welfare dependency in Japan could be rising soon.

25

What Are *Keiretsu* and Why Do Some U.S. Companies Dislike Them?

Gary S. Kikuchi

General Motors, General Electric, General Tire, and General Dynamics are well known U.S. corporations. Similarly, Mitsubishi Bank, Mitsubishi Corporation, Mitsubishi Heavy Industries, and Mitsubishi Motors are well known Japanese business firms. Some corporations share the same name because they share a common history (e.g., Westinghouse Electric and Westinghouse Air Brake). Others share the same name by coincidence (e.g., American Airlines, American Express, and American Fence) and may even do some business with each other, but are not affiliated. In contrast, the four Japanese corporations that share the Mitsubishi name, even though they are not in the same line of business, are part of a large group of affiliated companies. In Japan, such large groups are called *keiretsu*.

Horizontal versus Vertical *Keiretsu*

The Mitsubishi Group is a horizontal *keiretsu*. The horizontal *keiretsu* is a diverse group of companies that tend to borrow mainly from a primary lender (the main bank), hold one another's shares, and sometimes exchange personnel; the presidents, chief executives, and directors of the core corporations meet monthly. Presently there are six major horizontal *keiretsu* in Japan. Besides Mitsubishi (main bank—Mitsubishi Bank), the others are Mitsui (Sakura Bank), Sumitomo (Sumitomo Bank), Fuyo (Fuji Bank), Dai-Ichi-Kangyo (Dai-Ichi-Kangyo Bank), and Sanwa (Sanwa Bank).

The exact membership of each horizontal *keiretsu* is difficult to determine because individual corporations may be close to or distant from the core. The Mitsubishi Group, for example, has twenty-nine members in its core as identified by attendance at monthly meetings, and twenty-two of these corporations include the word "Mitsubishi" in their name. About 20 percent of the bank loans issued to these core firms in 1987 came from either the Mitsubishi Bank, Mitsubishi Trust and Banking, Meiji Mutual Life and Insurance, or Tokio Marine and Fire Insurance, all core members of the Mitsubishi Group. Mitsubishi Corporation, a trading company, is the chief distributor, exporter, and importer for the group. It buys about 20 percent of the goods and services produced by other members of the group, and about 10 percent of its sales are to other members of the group. On average, about 35 percent of the shares of any given member of the group is held by other members of the core group. If we include all the businesses that both borrow primarily from Mitsubishi Bank and have cross-holdings of shares with other members of the group, the number of affiliates increases to 217. But because many of these firms also deal with other *keiretsu*, it becomes increasingly difficult to classify the marginal firms as members of any particular *keiretsu*. Therefore, it is best to think only of the core group included in monthly meetings when we refer to a particular horizontal *keiretsu*.

The other type of *keiretsu* is the vertical *keiretsu*. A vertical *keiretsu* is a cluster of firms linked through the supply and distribution chains of a principal manufacturer. Toyota, the well-known automobile manufacturer, is an example of this type of *keiretsu*. Toyota itself belongs to Mitsui's bank, a major horizontal *keiretsu*. But Toyota deals mainly with the same parts suppliers and dealers which, in turn, deal either exclusively or principally with Toyota. This special relationship is a vertical *keiretsu*.

In 1991, Toyota Motors produced 4 million cars compared to the 3.7 million cars produced by General Motors. GM had 750,000 employees compared to 73,000 for Toyota. The large numerical difference in their employees is not because Toyota workers were 10 times as productive as GM workers; the explanation is that GM produces more than half of its auto parts in-house, whereas Toyota and other Japanese automobile companies buy most (about 80 percent) of their parts from other independent, but affiliated companies.

Toyota may also hold large blocks of shares in these companies. Cross-holding of stocks among Japanese corporations is common. In Japan less than 25 percent of corporate stocks is owned by individuals and about 65 percent of the stocks is owned by banks and other Japanese companies. (Foreign individuals and corporations own another 9 percent of Japanese corporate stocks.) By contrast, in the United States, more than 50 percent of corporate stocks are owned by individuals.

In addition to the first-tier parts suppliers that deal directly with Toyota, there are other parts suppliers that supply parts to the first-tier suppliers so that the firms connected to Toyota become quite extensive. Moreover, some parts suppliers may do substantial business with two or more *keiretsu*. Koito Manufacturing, for example, is a member of the Toyota Group but Honda also buys a substantial amount of its supplies from Koito. As in the case of the horizontal *keiretsu*, the membership in the vertical *keiretsu* becomes quite blurred, making it difficult to draw exact boundaries for the *keiretsu*.

Keiretsu and Capital Markets

How were these clusters of affiliated companies formed? Until recently, the Japanese government strictly regulated the domestic capital market. The Ministry of Finance exercised considerable influence on the lending policies of the banks, and prodded them to lend to firms in selected industries. Since the Japanese stock market was relatively underdeveloped due to heavy government restrictions, equity financing was relatively expensive and firms relied heavily on borrowing from the banks. The major banks naturally tended to lend to their preferred (often, prewar) customers. Likewise many of the firms that borrowed from the same bank had already developed strong ties with each other before World War II.

Some people believe that heavy reliance on loans instead of equity financing makes Japanese firms vulnerable to corporate takeovers. They believe extensive cross-holding of stocks among *keiretsu* members was designed as a defense mechanism against hostile takeovers by outsiders. In an episode that fueled frictions between Japan and the United States, T. Boone Pickens, an American venture capitalist, was unsuccessful in his attempt to gain a seat on the board of directors of Koito Manufacturing Company even though he was the company's largest single shareholder. Pickens alleged that Koito owed more allegiance to its *keiretsu* principal, Toyota Motor Company, also a major shareholder in Koito. Frustrated by his experience, Pickens sold his shares in Koito Manufacturing.

Some people believe that cross-shareholding helps cement long-term customer–vendor relationships among member firms. Others believe that its purpose is to make it possible for member firms to monitor one another, and thus prevent some members from engaging in overly risky actions. Still others believe that the purpose of cross-shareholding among *keiretsu* members is to conceal the true value of these companies.

Benefits of *Keiretsu* Membership

Whatever the reason for their coming into existence, *keiretsu* would not survive for long unless they offered sufficient benefits to their members. What could these benefits be?

Acquiring information about a company is very costly. Within a *keiretsu*, the main bank has the ability to acquire detailed insider information about the member firms who are its borrowers, and use this information to monitor the member companies closely and to influence their policies. Individual investors have neither the resources nor the skills to perform this function. With this insider information, the main bank is able to protect its own investment. Knowing that the main bank is monitoring the member companies, potential investors also feel more comfortable about investing in these companies. Thus, both the member firms and the bank benefit from such a relationship.

Because the main bank monitors the *keiretsu* firms closely, a long-term relationship becomes possible. Even if a member firm is facing short-term financial difficulties, the main bank may continue to lend money to it if the bank knows that the company is otherwise fundamentally sound. Without access to insider information, a bank might be reluctant to help such troubled companies.

By helping each other in times of trouble, members of a *keiretsu* can reduce their overall risk. The main bank may charge a lower interest rate, a trading company may extend more and longer-term credit, and a customer firm may offer a better price to a troubled member firm. When Mazda ran into trouble after choosing the rotary engine for its cars, Sumitomo Bank extended substantial credit and sent some key bank personnel to advise Mazda. Other members of the *keiretsu* encouraged their employees to buy Mazda cars, and vendors and dealers made large concessions to help Mazda out of its financial troubles.

Increased efficiency is another reason that is often cited as an advantage of the *keiretsu*. It is costly for a manufacturer to acquire information and to bargain and negotiate with its parts suppliers. One solution is to make the parts in-house. Thus, GM has its own, large in-house parts division. However, this makes GM a very large company. Critics argue that when a company becomes very large, it becomes inefficient and costs begin to rise sharply. A *keiretsu* can be seen as an intermediate status between the two extremes of either the total independence of a manufacturer from its parts suppliers or the total integration of the parts suppliers into the manufacturing company (i.e., consolidation into a single firm). Being in the middle, it can reap the benefits from both organizational arrangements. The *keiretsu* manufacturer, by holding substantial shares of its suppliers and having established long-term business relationships with them, doesn't face constant incurrence of the high costs of negotiating and contracting business among the parties. This arrangement also prevents the manufacturing company from becoming too large and inefficient since the parts suppliers are not a division of the manufacturing company.

The flip side of such long-term relationships is that some nonmember firms that are able to supply parts more cheaply may be denied a potential sale to the manufacturer.

Members of the *keiretsu* can also help each other by directing business opportunities to their affiliated firms. For example, Mitsubishi Corporation, a trading company, may discover while negotiating a contract to sell heavy machinery produced by Mitsubishi Heavy Industries, that the customer also wants to buy a fleet of cars. The trading company can also offer to sell cars built by Mitsubishi Motors.

Keiretsu and Market Power

Some critics of *keiretsu* believe that the advantage of *keiretsu* membership has less to do with increasing efficiency and more to do with consolidating market power for the members. It has been common practice for many electronics retailers to deal exclusively or primarily with one manufacturer. If a retailer has leftover shelf space, it may want to carry other manufacturers' brands. However, there have been many instances where dealers were prohibited from doing so because their main suppliers had threatened to cut off their own supplies and products. Does *keiretsu* improve efficiency or does it consolidate market power? There is no conclusive evidence to support either theory.

U.S. Criticism

Many Americans see *keiretsu* as a major impediment to U.S. companies trying to sell their products in Japan. U.S. automobile manufacturers allege that it is difficult for them to sell American cars in Japan, in part, because Japanese automobile dealers are afraid to display American cars in their showrooms for fear that the Japanese automobile companies will no longer supply cars to them. Kodak uses the same allegation to explain why its share of Japan's photo film market is lower, and Fuji's share is higher, than it should be. U.S. auto parts suppliers have complained vociferously that the Japanese automakers prefer to buy from their *keiretsu* members at higher prices. Statistical evidence shows that import penetration is lower in Japanese markets where *keiretsu* firms have large market shares. Japan's Economic Planning Agency agrees that *keiretsu* is a barrier to opening the Japanese markets to potential foreign competitors.

On the other hand, nobody complains when the manufacturing division of GM gives preference to parts made by its own parts division. If Toyota owns substantial shares of Koito, why should it be wrong for Toyota to depend heavily on Koito for its parts? Is there any reason to believe that it's okay for GM to use mainly parts produced by its in-house parts division, but Toyota should be condemned for using parts made by a supplier of which Toyota has significant ownership?

In Japan, where long-term business relationships are the norm, newcomers to a market are at a distinct competitive disadvantage. Since these newcomers are often foreign companies trying to break into the Japanese markets, they find entry difficult because of long-standing business relationships among financially affiliated Japanese firms. While we often hear reports from the news media that foreign companies are shut out of Japanese markets because they are foreign, a better explanation is that they are new to the Japanese markets and, because Japanese business relationships are built on long-term commitments, it is difficult for newcomers to break into the market.

The Future of *Keiretsu*

The *keiretsu* structure is beginning to show some cracks in its armor. The formidable Japanese banks that once formed the nucleus of the six big horizontal *keiretsu* find themselves in deep trouble as they struggle to stay afloat in Japan's increasingly deregulated financial environment. Many member firms that once relied on the main bank for financing are now finding alternative sources of capital. Some cash-rich companies, such as Toyota, don't have to rely on any banks for financing. Not surprisingly, Toyota has begun to distance itself from Sakura Bank. Saddled with huge portfolios of bad loans made during the bubble-economy years of the late 1980s, the main banks no longer have the resources or the willingness to keep weak member companies financially afloat.

The collapse of the Japanese bubble economy after 1990 and the recession that followed have increased the costs of maintaining long-term relationships among member firms. With sales and profits declining, member companies are not as willing to buy supplies at higher prices from another member company and instead are increasingly buying their supplies from and selling their outputs to nonmember companies. Thus, the economic glue that held the membership together in the past has weakened as short-run survival has taken priority over maintaining long-term relationships. Deregulation and more vigorous enforcement of Japan's Anti-Monopoly Law also appear to have delivered a blow to the *keiretsu*.

On the other hand, in 1997 Japan's parliament lifted the postwar ban against holding companies in order to promote greater economic efficiency. Holding companies hold shares in other companies and control those companies' operations. While they are common in the United States and in Europe, they were banned by the U.S. occupation forces out of concern about possible reemergence of pre–World War II financial cliques (giant conglomerate companies known as *zaibatsu*) which had controlled Japan. As a result, some believe that the *keiretsu* links may become stronger in the future. At this point, it is unclear whether the influence of the *keiretsu* in the Japanese economy will grow stronger or become weaker.

26

Is Japan an Egalitarian Society?

Harry T. Oshima

Early one morning while walking in Shinjuku, Tokyo, I saw cops waking up the homeless sleeping on the sidewalk in front of a big department store. The cops ordered them to pick up their blankets and cardboards and get moving. Apparently, the homeless were allowed to sleep there during the night but at the crack of dawn they were supposed to disappear.

Japan had large numbers of poor people before World War II, but their number fell dramatically after the war. The number of poor households dropped from 33 percent of the total in 1963 to only 5 percent in 1977. With a prolonged period of rapid economic growth, poverty was virtually wiped out in Japan by the end of the 1980s (see chapter 24).

Income is more equally divided among the Japanese than among Americans. In 1993, the share of total family income in Japan that went to the richest 20 percent of the families was 5 times the share that went to the poorest 20 percent of the families (39 percent versus 8 percent). In the United States, the ratio was nearly 12 times (46 percent versus 4 percent).

Thus, a comparison of family income distributions shows that Japan is a more egalitarian society than the United States. Today,

Distribution of Family Income:
Japan versus United States
(1993)

	Percentage of Total Family Income	
Nation's Families	Japan	United States
Richest 20%	39	46
Next highest 20%	23	24
Middle 20%	17	16
Next lowest 20%	13	10
Poorest 20%	8	4
	100	100

Japan has the most equal distribution of income among industrialized countries.

How Is It That Income Is So Equally Shared in Japan?

Ironically, part of the answer to this question goes back to the fact that the victorious U.S. occupation forces in the late 1940s forced Japan to undertake a comprehensive program for the democratization of the country. As a result, the rich families lost control of their big farms and big companies. Land reform was successfully implemented, and tenants and landless farm workers received land and gained control of farm cooperatives and other agricultural institutions. Labor unions were legalized and, with the support of the government, workers were able to gain dramatic increases in wages. A progressive income tax system was enacted, credit was made accessible to small businesses, and nine years of free education was made available to all children.

With industries and agriculture revitalized, per capita income grew rapidly, averaging nearly 6 percent increase per year between the 1960s and the 1980s compared to less than 2 percent increase per year in the United States. Japanese worker productivity grew much faster than in the United States—5.6

percent per year in Japan compared to 0.5 percent per year in
the United States. Productivity rose in large part because Japanese workers were willing to work long hours (see chapters 13
and 15). Compared to other industrialized countries, a much
larger percentage of the elderly (those sixty-five years and over)
in Japan continued to work after retirement.

Families in Japan saved much more than American families
(see chapter 16), making it possible to use those savings to
mechanize farms and to finance rapid industrialization. Part of
the savings went toward the education of the young, enabling
them to acquire better skills.

High rates of economic growth produced full employment
in the 1950s and kept the economy at full employment through
the 1980s. During this period Japan's unemployment rate averaged only 2 percent compared to 6 percent in the United
States. Prolonged full employment pushed up wages of un-
skilled laborers and working wives, raising the incomes of the
lower 40 percent of the nation's families.

My own experience during this period in Japan illustrates the
growing shortage of labor in the Japanese labor market. My
family was living in Tokyo during the late 1950s, and we were
able to hire a live-in maid from the countryside. But she left for
a factory job the following year, and we could only find a housewife who was willing to come to work for a couple of hours in
the morning and afternoon. But she, too, left after a while, and
my wife had to do the housework in the last year of our stay.
Housemaids had by then become practically an extinct species
in the Japanese labor market.

Despite land reform, incomes on the farms were much lower
than in the cities. In the 1960s, labor shortages in the cities
forced small manufacturing firms to move to the rural areas to
find workers; the men left the farms for factories, leaving farm
work to their wives. Income earned from factory jobs soon out-
stripped income earned from the farms. The number of farm
households decreased rapidly and farming became a part-time
activity (see chapter 20). This migration of factories to the rural

areas helped equalize income between farm and city and among the farm families. This was a major factor contributing to income equalization in Japan as a whole.

Pay Equity in Japanese Companies

In a recent survey of thirty major U.S. corporations, the *Wall Street Journal* found that average compensation of their chief executive officers (CEOs) was 212 times that of the average American employee. (Thirty years ago it was 44 times!) Similar studies show that the ratio is only about 16 for Japan and 21 for Germany. This is not to say that the Japanese pay system is particularly egalitarian—especially if you add the very generous executive fringe benefits such as large expense accounts and housing and automobile allowances. It is the American executive compensation system that is in a category of its own.

A Hierarchical Society

By other criteria, Japan is *not* an egalitarian society. Most, if not all social relationships in Japan are hierarchical. This is true of families, workplaces, and political, cultural, and social organizations. Relatively strict norms govern interpersonal relationships between superiors and subordinates, between senior and junior members of an organization (based on the date of entry), and between patrons and clients. While such status and rank differentials also exist in Western societies, they are more widely recognized and rigidly observed in Japan. The rank-conscious Japanese must always be on the alert when meeting strangers in order that proper social etiquette be observed. Indeed, one of the purposes of the common practice of exchanging business cards *(meishi)* in Japan is to inform the receiver of the rank of the giver so that each person knows the proper social etiquette.

Among other things, relative rank determines the proper language and manner of speaking used by each person.

Japan's hierarchical social order is a holdover from the Tokugawa feudal society with its adherence to Confucian teachings, which demand filial piety from sons to their fathers, from younger brothers to their older brothers, obedience from wife to the husband, and loyalty from the ruled to the ruler. It contrasts sharply with the egalitarian heritage of the frontier days in nineteenth-century America.

Nonetheless, within this hierarchical society, decisions are not made by a majority that may trample over the rights of the minority. The superior, the senior, and the patron cannot act arbitrarily but must respect the views of others, and will usually yield to subordinates when his views are not acceptable to most of the others. Consensus is reached through long, drawn-out discussion with broad participation and consultation. Because of the importance of group decision-making, Japanese companies hold lots of conferences/meetings; two meetings a day or over ten per week are not unusual. In Japan, policy changes are often initiated from the middle and lower echelons of the management hierarchy, not from the top down. Managers and workers in Japan wear the same uniform, eat at the same cafeteria, and work at the same size desks all located in one large room.

Unequal Treatment of Women

Women face separate and often unequal treatment relative to men in many aspects of Japanese everyday life. In the workplace, Japanese women face tougher obstacles than American women in getting fair treatment in recruiting, hiring, job assignment, promotion, and pay equity with men. Women are generally tracked into dead-end jobs with few meaningful responsibilities and little prospect of promotion. The average wage among female workers is only 62 percent of the average male wage in

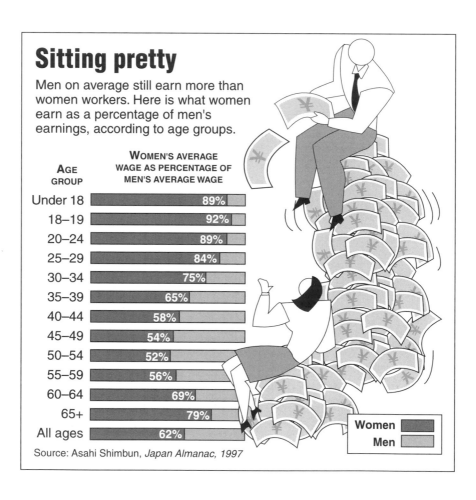

Sitting pretty

Men on average still earn more than women workers. Here is what women earn as a percentage of men's earnings, according to age groups.

AGE GROUP	WOMEN'S AVERAGE WAGE AS PERCENTAGE OF MEN'S AVERAGE WAGE
Under 18	89%
18–19	92%
20–24	89%
25–29	84%
30–34	75%
35–39	65%
40–44	58%
45–49	54%
50–54	52%
55–59	56%
60–64	69%
65+	79%
All ages	62%

Women
Men

Source: Asahi Shimbun, *Japan Almanac, 1997*

Japan, compared to 71 percent in the United States. Japan's Labor Standards Law also contains a discriminatory "female protective provision" that restricts women from working overtime, on holidays, or late at night. Forty-six percent of the women polled recently replied that their companies pushed women to quit when they became pregnant or after they gave birth.

The Equal Employment Opportunity Law (EEOL) was passed in 1985 to advance the economic progress of Japanese working women—despite widespread public opposition to the proposed law. Many Japanese believed that gender equity would lead to the collapse of the nation's culture and its values. The law, however, did not provide sufficient enforcement mechanism and sanctions to ensure that employers would comply with the law. Ten years after its passage, the Ministry of Labor observed that the EEOL "has changed the rules but not the conditions." Revisions to the EEOL are under consideration.

Women lag behind men in university attendance as well. While at Hitotsubashi University near Tokyo in the late 1950s, I found only one female student enrolled. When I asked her how she found life at Hitotsubashi, she replied that it wasn't very convenient. For example, there were no separate toilets for women, and when in a hurry, she had to run to the nearby bushes. More recently, I attended an economics conference at Hitotsubashi University (March 1997) and learned that women comprised only 15 percent of its student body. After three decades, progress in gender equity at the university has been quite slow.

In 1995, 41 percent of male high school graduates in Japan advanced to universities, compared to 23 percent of female graduates. In contrast, nearly 25 percent of the female high

school graduates advanced to junior colleges, compared to 2 percent of male graduates. While the percentage of students advancing to higher education (junior college and university combined) was higher for females than for males, female graduates were far more likely to go to junior colleges while male graduates overwhelmingly chose to go to universities.

One explanation for this difference in higher education attendance between males and females is that in Japan parents tend to assign higher priority to sending their sons to universities. Another, and perhaps related, explanation is that given the discrimination that women in Japan face in the job market, the return on investment in a university education is much higher for men than for women. During the recent economic recession, female university graduates found it much harder to find a regular full-time job than male university graduates.

Curiously, at the Hitotsubashi University conference I attended, there were no women among the Japanese participants. By contrast, half of the Taiwan participants were women.

Minorities, the Aged, the Handicapped, and Other Disadvantaged

The concept of human rights exists only vaguely in Japan. Koreans, the Ainu (Japan's indigenous people), and other ethnic minorities face widespread economic and social discrimination. Overall there may be less minority discrimination in Japan than in the United States, but only because of the country's relative ethnic homogeneity.

Japanese labor laws do not protect the elderly against employment discrimination. Employment ads commonly specify age limits for job openings. Mandatory retirement age is part of the work culture, with most employers requiring their workers to retire between the ages of fifty-five and sixty. In 1986, the government passed legislation (Retirement-at-Sixty Law) suggesting a retirement age of sixty for Japanese workers. Today, more than two-thirds of Japanese companies impose a mandatory retirement age of sixty. Faced with a rapidly aging population, the Ministry of Labor proposes to raise the suggested retirement age to sixty-five.

There is much less public help for the handicapped and disabled in Japan than in the United States. Don't bother to look for wheelchair-accessible buses, trains, and public bathrooms, or wheelchair ramps in public buildings and sidewalks. If you are in a wheelchair and have to climb down (up) those nosebleed inducing and ear-popping steep stairs in some Japanese train stations, you have to depend on the kindness of fellow passengers or available train station attendants to carry you down (up) the stairs so you can ride the trains. Then you have to depend on other compassionate passengers or station attendants to help you up (down) the stairs at the destination. It's not so easy to find help when everyone at the train stations appears to be in a hurry to get somewhere, especially during the rush hours.

In Japan, inheritance usually goes to the firstborn son. The other siblings get little, if anything, despite laws to the contrary.

Japan's educational system is often mentioned as a symbol of its egalitarian society. Entrance to the best and most prestigious schools is determined solely on the basis of competitive examinations. However, the rising cost of cram schools (see chapter 3), which prepare students to perform well on school entrance examinations, increasingly exclude children of lower-income families. Besides having the money to pay the tuition at the most expensive cram schools, students from high-income families also have other advantages in gaining admission to the most prestigious schools. The *Asahi Shimbun* (November 27, 1991) reported that the average annual family income of students at the most prestigious university in Japan—Tokyo University—exceeded 10 million yen compared to the average annual family income in Japan of around 7 million yen (excluding agricultural, fishery, and single-member households). More than half of the parents of Tokyo University students held administrative or managerial jobs.

What Is an Egalitarian Society?

It may be for these reasons that the noted sociologist Chie Nakane thinks of Japanese society not as the pejorative "hierarchical" society but the more neutral "vertical" society. In sum, whether or not Japan is an egalitarian society depends on your definition, what evidence you look at, and how you weigh the evidence. In comparison to America, Japan exhibits far more equality of income and (for males, at least) workplace participation, but there may be less social equality.

GLOSSARY OF JAPANESE TERMS

aotagai   practice of hiring students before the date agreed on among employers and universities. Lit., "to harvest green rice"

awamori   Okinawa distilled rice spirits

bon; obon   three-day, midsummer all souls' festival with its associated Buddhist rites

chōwa   harmony

chūgen; ochūgen   midsummer gifts given to those of superior or equal status and not within a family

dokushin kizoku   "bachelor royalty"; young persons who live at home and use earnings for their own pleasure and benefit

gaiatsu   pressure from abroad; foreign influence

gaikoku seihin   Western-made goods

giri   duty or moral obligation to carry out one's obligations

giri choco   duty chocolate given by females to male colleagues, co-workers, etc.

gohan   cooked rice; food

gyōsei-shidō   "discretionary guidance," such as advice offered by the Ministry of Finance to commercial banks

hanko   chop, seal, used with red-ink pad to make a seal on paper; used in place of a signature

hoshōkin   combined key money and rental deposit paid to landlords/apartment owners

ibiri   harassment at the workplace

ijime   hazing, harassment among schoolchildren; bullying

jitan sokushin ryōkin   fee for promoting shorter hours

juku   cram school

kachō   section head

karōshi   death from overwork

keiretsu   affiliated company groups

konbini   convenience stores

kyōiku-mama   mother who is obsessed with her children's education

kyōyōbu   "general education" or core requirement courses for university students

maruyū   tax-exempt

meishi   business cards; calling cards

nenkō   wage system adjusted for age and duration of employment

omamori   good-luck charms as gifts brought back from a trip

omiyage   souvenir gifts

pachinko   Japanese pinball machine

rāmen   Chinese-style soup noodles

reikin   nonrefundable key money paid to a landlord to rent an apartment or house

seibo; oseibo   year-end gifts

seiyō sūhai   Western worship; strong desire for and emulation of Western things and manners

senbetsu   send-off monetary gift given to those going on trips

shikikin   rental deposit

shinki gakusotsu ikkatsu saiyō   one-shot or "shot-gun" hiring of new graduates

shuntō   Spring Offensive; spring labor negotiations

sumō   Japanese wrestling

taraimawashi   practice of passing on gifts to another person

teigaku deposit certificates   term or time deposit certificates

tokubetsu yōgo rōjin hōmu   special nursing home for the elderly

yobikō   special schools that prepare young people to take college entrance examinations *yokonarabi*   "level behavior"; cooperation to avoid excessive competition

zaibatsu   pre–World War II giant conglomerate companies and financial cliques

SOURCES FOR STATISTICAL DATA ON JAPAN

The following data sources on Japan are recommended to those who read only English.

In Print

Government of Japan, Management and Coordination Agency, Statistics Bureau, *Japan Statistical Yearbook, 1997* (Tokyo: October 1996). ISBN 4-8223-1846-x-0093.

The official government statistical data book. Write to: Mainichi Newspaper, 1-1-1 Hitotsubashi, Chiyoda-ku, Tokyo 100-51, Japan. (Price: About 14,500 yen.)

Asahi Shimbun, *Japan Almanac, 1997* (Tokyo: October 1996), ISBN 4-02-219597-5

An excellent annual publication containing data in thirty fields. Write to: Asahi Shimbun, 5-3-2 Tsukiji, Chuo-ku, Tokyo 104-11, Japan. (Price: About 1,600 yen.)

Japan External Trade Organization (JETRO), *Nippon, 1996, Business Facts and Figures* (Tokyo, 1996), ISBN 4-8224-0751-9

An annual booklet containing mostly business and economic data. Write to: Japan External Trade Organization (JETRO), 2-5, Toranomon 2-chome, Minatoku, Tokyo 105, Japan. (Price: About 1,200 yen.)

Keizai Koho Center, *Japan 1997, An International Comparison* (Tokyo: Japan Institute for Social and Economic Affairs, December 1996). ISBN 4-87605-027-9

A pocket-size annual statistical publication comparing Japan with other countries. Write to: Keizai Koho Center, 6-1, Otemachi 1-chome, Chiyoda-ku, Tokyo 100, Japan. (Price: About 900 yen.)

On the Web

Government of Japan, Management and Co-ordination Agency, Statistics Bureau, *Japan in Figures, 1997.*
Web site: http://www.stat.go.jp/1611.htm

Japan Information Network, *Statistics.*
Web site: http://www.jinjapan.org/stat/

This web site also has links to other Japanese and international statistical resources.

ABOUT THE CONTRIBUTORS

Shigeyuki Abe is Professor of Economics at the Research Institute for Economics and Business Administration, Kobe University (Japan), and coeditor of this volume.

Yoshitaka Fukui is a Ph.D. candidate in business (accounting) at Carnegie Mellon University (USA). He received his undergraduate law degree at the University of Tokyo in 1985.

Teruyuki Higa (deceased) was Professor of Economics at Okinawa International University (Japan).

Susumu Hondai is Professor of Economics in the Graduate School of International Co-operation Studies, Kobe University.

Charles Yuji Horioka is Associate Professor at the Institute for Social and Economic Research, Osaka University (Japan).

Kazuhiro Igawa is Professor of Economics at the Research Institute for Economics and Business Administration, Kobe University, and coeditor of this volume.

Toshiki Jinushi is Professor of Economics in the Faculty of Economics, Kobe University.

Akihiko Kawaura is Associate Professor of Economics at Otaru University (Japan).

Gary Kikuchi is Adjunct Instructor of Economics at Syracuse University (USA).

Yoko Kimura is Associate Professor of Public Economics at Nara Women's University (Japan).

Sumner LaCroix is Professor of Economics at the University of Hawaii at Manoa (USA).

Matthew Loke is Research Analyst at the Hawaii Medical Services Association, Blue Cross-Blue Shield and Adjunct Faculty at Hawaii Pacific University (USA).

Karen Lupardus is Professor of English at Okinawa International University.

James Mak is Professor of Economics at the University of Hawaii at Manoa, and coeditor of this volume.

Robert McCleery is Visiting Associate Professor of Economics at Claremont McKenna College (USA).

Andrew Mason is Professor of Economics at the University of Hawaii at Manoa and Research Associate at the East-West Center, Honolulu.

Naoki Mitani is Professor of Economics in the Faculty of Economics at Kobe University.

Shoji Nishijima is Professor of Economics at the Research Institute of Economics and Business Administration at Kobe University.

Kazuo Nishiyama is Professor of Intercultural Communication at the University of Hawaii at Manoa.

Naohiro Ogawa is Professor and Deputy Director of the Population Research Institute at Nihon University (Japan).

Harry Oshima is Professor (emeritus) of Economics at the University of Hawaii at Manoa and Visiting Fellow at the East-West Center.

Robert Parry is Lecturer in the Faculty of Economics, Kobe University.

Shyam Sunder is Richard M. Cyert Professor of Management and Economics at Carnegie Mellon University, and coeditor of this volume.

Index

aging society: health care, 164–165; savings, 118–119

agriculture. *See* farmers; households

ATMs (automatic teller machines), 60–61, 137–147. *See also* banks

automobiles, 49, 191, 198

Bank of Japan, 144, 146

banks, 59, 62–63, 64–65, 167–171; branches of, 145, 167, 170; checking accounts at, 59–66, 146–147, 169; children's banks, 118; competition among, 63–64, 144, 146–147, 169; credit cards and, 64; electronic transfer at, 60, 63–64, 175, 176; employees of, 139–142; interest rates of, 146, 168. *See also* ATMs; government regulation; *keiretsu;* Postal Savings Office

banks (private): Dai-Ichi-Kangyo, 167, 186; Fuji Bank, 143–144, 186; Sakura Bank, 140, 186, 192; Sanwa Bank, 141, 145, 186; Sumitomo Bank, 141, 143–145, 186; Tokyo-Mitsubishi, 167, 186

bonuses, 42, 99–100, 102–103; and savings, 118; and social security, 158

brand-name goods, 30, 39–43, 51

bubble economy, 42, 49, 56, 192

bullying, 25. *See also* workplace harassment

cash-oriented society, 60–61, 62, 140, 147; concealment of noncash costs, 163–165

checking accounts. *See* banks

children, 13–17; childless marriages, 13; and pachinko, 35, 37; and savings, 118; on welfare, 179, 181. *See also* education

cities: Beijing, 38; Hong Kong, 56; Honolulu, 56, 39, 52, 56, 149; Kobe, ix, 45, 52, 55, 141, 176; Kyoto, 45, 55; Las Vegas, 34, 36, 38; Los Angeles, 56; Nagoya, 34; New York, 55, 63, 111–112; Osaka, 45, 50, 55; San Francisco, 56; Seoul, 56; Tokyo, 37, 48, 50, 54, 55, 56, 111–113, 140, 197

collective bargaining, 93, 100, 102. *See also* labor unions

commuting, 6, 110–111

companies, affiliated. See *keiretsu*

competition, avoidance of, 65, 126, 138, 191. *See also* banks; vending machines

Confucian teachings, 117, 199

Constitution, 181

consumer, 49, 66, 117–118, 155; protection, 7

cram schools. *See* education, *juku*

credit cards, 61–62, 64, 140

crime: Aum Shinrikyo, 140; low rate of, 7, 62–63, 124, 140, 164; organized, 37; pachinko, 37–38; of vandalism, 125, 142

death from overwork, 107

deregulation, 43, 49–50, 170, 192. *See also* government regulation

development, regional, 169

discount stores. *See* retail stores, discount

215

distribution system, 49
drugs (pharmaceuticals), 134–135

earnings, 79; age–wage curve,
    103–104; of CEOs, 198; compensa-
    tion system, 100; and education,
    78–79; household, 55; and seniority,
    86–87; wages, 93, 196. *See also* over-
    time; universities; women
economic growth: household savings
    in proportion to, 117, 119; post-war,
    8, 125, 169, 171, 181, 196, 197; slow-
    down, 80, 118
education: bullying *(ijime)* in, 25; cost
    of, 23–24, 203; education mother
    and, 15; and entrance examinations,
    15, 23, 25–26, 73, 203; and govern-
    ment subsidy, 22; *juku* (cram
    school), 15, 21–26, 203; Ministry of
    Education (Monbusho), 21, 26; pub-
    lic, 73, 196, 197; system of, 21–22, 40;
    truancy (school refusal syndrome),
    25. *See also* earnings; universities
elderly, 16–17, 181, 183, 197; age dis-
    crimination and the, 104, 202; care
    of, 13, 16; and health care plan, 159;
    in hospitals, 161; on welfare, 179,
    181. *See also* aging society
election districts, 53
employment: age discrimination and,
    86, 104; civil service, 83; contract
    hiring, 81, 90; employee benefits of,
    70; employers and, 76, 90; hiring sys-
    tem, 83–90; lifetime employment,
    83, 88, 90; part-time, 15, 55, 83, 90;
    seniority in, 85–86, 88. *See also* earn-
    ings; workers; unemployment
exchange rate, 3 n.; market exchange
    rate, 4–5

family: income, 196; legal obligations
    to, 181; in multi-generational house-
    holds, 55, 183; traditional, 12–13,
    181

farmers: cooperatives, 151, 196; farm
    mechanization, 197; land reform,
    196; loans, 169; lobby, 52–53, 153;
    part-time, 149; political power, 151,
    153, 155; taxation, 69–70. *See also*
    government regulation; income; rice
festivals, 27–28
food, 51, 53, 152. *See also* rice; vending
    machines
foreign companies: entry barriers to,
    49, 191; foreign retailers and, 50;
    perception of, 87
foreigners, in Japan, 54, 61, 64
frugality, 117, 181
funerals, 29–30, 180, 182

gambling, 36
GATT (General Agreement on Tariffs
    and Trade), 53, 154
GDP (gross domestic product), 3–6,
    7–8, 132, 157–158
gift-giving, 27–32, 40–41; between co-
    workers, 29, 31, 41; cash, 30–31; cor-
    porate, 31–32; funerals, 29–30, 31;
    souvenirs, 28–29, 30, 41; unwanted
    gifts, 31; weddings, 29–30, 31
golf, 36, 70
government, local, 181
government, operating costs. *See* taxes,
    administrative costs of
governmental agencies: Economic
    Planning Agency, 96; Japanese Food
    Agency, 150–151, 155
government regulation: and agricul-
    tural industry, 56, 153; and con-
    sumer prices, 8–9, 49; of domestic
    capital, 187; of financial institutions,
    142–144, 192, 193; of health care,
    57, 133–134, 158–160; and land
    prices, 56, 125; of retail stores, 47–
    50. *See also* deregulation; farmers;
    rice
group orientation, 76, 85, 199

handicapped, 8, 179, 203

harmony, 32. *See also* gift-giving

health care: expenditures, 57–58, 157–165; factors influencing, 163–164; and GDP, 157–158; government control of, 133, 158; limitations on coverage, 158–159. *See also* medical care

health insurance, 15, 57, 131–132

holding companies, 193

homeless, 195

households: agricultural, 197; expenditures in, 51–58; in poverty, 195; savings of, 115–120; savings decrease in, 118–119

housewives. *See* wives

housework: husband's contribution, 13

housing: apartments and condominiums, 54–56; comparison of cost with U.S., 7; cost, 10, 17, 51, 54–57; and household savings, 117; PHLC (housing loans) and, 169–170; size of, 10, 26, 46, 95; subsidy for, 70, 180

imports, agricultural, 52–55; restrictions on, 8, 42, 43

income: after taxes, 51; equalization of, 198, 204; family, 196; farm, 197

infrastructure, public. *See* social infrastructure

inheritance, 203

insurance. *See* health insurance; social security

IRS (Internal Revenue Service), 67

juku. See education, *juku*

karaoke, 129

keiretsu, 31, 185–193; benefits from, 188–190; capital markets, 187–188; market share, 191; structure of, 185–187

Koreans, 33

labor costs, 124–125

labor force, 73

labor market, 77, 80, 84

labor-shortage environment, 93

labor unions, 84, 100–101, 105, 196. *See also* collective bargaining

land prices, 56, 124

laws and acts: Anti-Monopoly Law, 192; Control and Improvement of Amusement Business, 36; Department Store Law (1947), 48; Equal Employment Opportunity Law (1985), 200–201, Food Control Act (1942), 150, 153; Fundamental Law of Education, 22; Labor Standards Law, 95, 111, 200; Large-Scale Retail Store Law (1973), 48, 49, 50; Retirement-at-Sixty Law (1986), 202; Staple Food Act (1942), 151

leisure, 6, 35–36, 89

literacy, 73, 139

litter, 128

manufacturing. *See* workers

marriage, 11–19, arranged, 12; conflict with work, 15; delayed, 11, 14; divorce, 7, 13; as metaphor for employment, 85; wedding costs, 17–18. *See also* education; children

medical care: costs of, 32, 57, 131, 158, 162; economic considerations of, 162; excessive medication as, 131–132; government control of, 57; hospitals and, 161–162; household spending on, 51; physicians and patients in, 132–133, 161; quality of, 163; welfare assistance for, 181. *See also* health care; health insurance

Meiji Restoration, 40, 149

middle class. *See* social status

Ministry of: Construction, 170; Education, 21, 26, 73, 80; Finance, 38, 110, 138, 143–146, 169, 187; Health and

Welfare (MOHW), 127, 133–135, 160, 161; Justice, 38; Labor, 91, 201, 203; Posts and Telecommunications, 167–168, 177; Trade and Industry (MITI), 48

minors: use of alcohol and cigarettes by, 128

money transfers. *See* banks; Postal Savings Office

monopoly, 142, 169; Antitrust Committee (AC), 143

National Land Agency survey, 55, 56

national security, 150

newspapers, 175, 182

NHK (public broadcasting), 173–177; as compared to Hawaii, 173–174; funding of, 174–175, 177; governmental control of, 174, 177; public attitudes toward, 176–177

NTT (Nippon Telephone and Telecommunications), 142

nursing homes, 16, 161–162. *See also* elderly

OECD (Organization for Economic Cooperation and Development), 4, 147

office ladies (OLs), 39, 43, 86, 109, 111

Okinawa, 123, 126, 150

opportunity costs versus lost wages, 78

overtime: by financial institutions, 109; legal restrictions on, 95, 200; management perception of, 95; service overtime, 6, 91–97, 109; workers' perception of, 94–95

pachinko, 33–38

police, 37–38, 195

Postal Savings Office (PSO), 59–60, 64–65, 137, 167–171; ATMs, 168; competition between banks and, 167, 169, 171; "Second National

Budget" and, 169; housing loans from, 169–170; interest rates of the, 168

pressure from abroad, 9

prices: compared to U.S., 4–5, 8, 42; food, 52–54, 153. *See also* government regulation, land

public broadcasting. *See* NHK

railways, 141, 203. *See also* train schedules

Rengo. *See* labor unions

retail stores, 46–50, 127; convenience stores and, 46, 59; discount, 46, 49; foreign, 50

retirement: age of, 203; lump-sum payments at, 100, 104

rice, 52, 149–155; decline in consumption of, 152; government control of, 150–152; price support of, 151–152; prices as a result of Uruguay Round of GATT, 154; quota on rice land, 150. *See also* government regulation

salarymen, 35, 55, 60, 86, 110, 113–114

savings: household, 51, 115–120, 197; of other countries, 6, 11, 120; promotion of, 118. *See also* frugality

schools, public, 114. *See also* education

self-employment. *See* workers

Shinto, 164

shopping, 39, 45, 51, 59, 99

signatures, 64

Singapore, 38; Singaporeans, 11

social conditions, 7–8

social control, 86

social infrastructure, 6–7, 170

social insurance health care model, 158

social mobility, 24, 32

social security, 15, 47, 181; and its effect on household savings, 117–118 social status: and gift-giving, 30, 41; hierarchical relationships and, 198, 199; middle-class, 30–31; souvenirs as indication of, 28–29, 30, 41; standard of living and, 5–10; stock market and, 188

Structural Impediments Initiative (1989), 49

supermarkets, 48

taxes, 67–70, 196; administrative costs of, 69, 177; consumption tax (national), 70; farmland, 56; individual tax returns, 67–70; and savings, 117–118; on wife's earnings, 15; withholding system of, 68–69

technological leap-frog theory, 63–64

television, public. See NHK

tipping, x

trade surplus, 8

training: OJT (on-the-job), 77; welfare assistance for, 181

train schedules, 110–113

transportation: household expenditure on, 51, 57–58; public, 47

travel: domestic, 28–29; foreign destinations, 13, 43, 86; reservations at convenience shops, 46; young women who, 16, 42. See also commuting; gift-giving; transportation

unemployment, 7, 197

unions, enterprise, 84, 100. See also labor unions

universities, 73–81; cost, 78; rate of graduation, 75; students, 74–75, 85; tenure of faculty at, 77–78; weakness of the system at, 76–78

vending machines, 50, 123–129, 142; competition for, 126–127; and crime, 125, 129; restrictions on, 128

voters, 53

wages. See earnings

welfare assistance, 10, 179–183; as compared to U.S., 180; and dependent children, 179; for health care, 159; qualifications for, 180

Western worship, 40

wives, 47, 60, 113, 176; in agriculture, 197; and care of elderly, 17; and obedience, 199; and pachinko, 35

women: and care of elderly, 17, 181; earnings of, 104, 199; employment discrimination toward, 7, 199, 202; higher education and, 16, 201; job opportunities for, 14, 201; marketing to, 128; office workers, 42, 43; traveling abroad, 16, 42; and welfare, 179

workers: as compared to U.S., 6; loyalty to firm, 93; manufacturing, 107–109, 113; productivity of, 196–197; salarymen, 21, 35; seasonal, 83; self-employed, 70, 83, 158. See also gift-giving

work ethic, instilled in children, 23

working conditions, 31, 139, 200

working hours, 6, 13, 197; pre-WWII, 107; reduction of, 96; surveys, 91–92. See also overtime

working wives, 15, 24, 55, 197; and motherhood, 200. See also marriage; office ladies; wives

workplace harassment, 96

youth, 118